"I truly believe that the format, content, and structure of this book is so dramatically different from the traditional genre of books about reading research and theory building that it has the potential to bring about a Kuhnian revolution in reading research and theory development on a number of levels. . . . Instead of tediously presenting research findings and interpreting what they *mean* for reading educators, this book leads its readers on a journey which subtly *persuades* them to explore and examine their own and others' reading behavior in ways that induce deeper understandings of the complexity of human symbolic behavior in general and the act of reading in particular. . . . I'm hopeful that this book will mark the beginning of a movement to rework reading and learning to read using the tools and perspectives from a wide range of more successful scientific disciplines."

Brian Cambourne, University of Wollongong,
Australia, From the Foreword

"Exciting and timely for the field. . . . This book guides the reader in exploring the processes of reading in ways that challenge common sense views and that have important pedagogical consequences. I love the dialogue. It sounds genuine and creates a kind of conversation space. The book is clearly focused on an important topic—it follows nicely the rule of keeping the main idea the main idea."

James Hoffman, University of Texas at Austin, USA

"A significant contribution to the field via a powerful theme, 'The Grand Illusion,' explored in a fashion that is multi-perspectival and multidisciplinary. Using a combination of expertise (language, psychology, physiology), the book makes a unique contribution pulling together research findings from various sources, fields of studies, and windows for observing the acts of reading (retellings, miscue analysis, eye movement, text analysis, and linguistic corpus). It provides a more coherent and provocative discussion than some of the government-commissioned/sponsored reports and reviews included in edited handbook volumes on reading."

Robert J. Tierney, University of British Columbia,
Canada; University of Sydney, Australia; and
Beijing Normal University, China

# Reading—The Grand Illusion

What is reading? In this groundbreaking book, esteemed researchers Ken Goodman, Peter H. Fries, and Steven L. Strauss explain not only what reading really is but also why common sense makes it seem to be something quite different from that reality. How can this *grand illusion* be explained? That is the purpose of this book. As the authors show, unraveling the secrets of the grand illusion of reading teaches about far more than reading itself, but also about how remarkable human language is, how the brain uses language to navigate the world, what it means to be human.

Each author brings a different perspective, but all share a common view of the reading process. Together they provide a clear and surprising exposition of the reading process, in which they involve readers of this book in exploring the ways they themselves read and make sense of written language while their eyes fixate on fewer than 70 percent of the words in the text. In addition, the authors engage in a cross-disciplinary discussion about how readers use the brain, eyes, and language in reading. The different perspectives provide depth to the authors' description of reading. The information presented in this book will be new to many teachers, researchers, teacher educators, and the public alike. The final chapter draws on the understandings from the book to challenge the treatment of reading and writing as school subjects and offers the basis for supporting literacy development as a natural extension of oral language development.

**Ken Goodman** is Professor Emeritus, Reading, Language and Culture, University of Arizona, USA.

**Peter H. Fries** is Professor Emeritus, Central Michigan University, USA.

**Steven L. Strauss** Ph.D and M.D. is a Neurologist, Private Practice, USA.

# Reading—The Grand Illusion

## How and Why People Make Sense of Print

KEN GOODMAN
PETER H. FRIES
STEVEN L. STRAUSS

Routledge
Taylor & Francis Group
NEW YORK AND LONDON

First published 2016
by Routledge
711 Third Avenue, New York, NY 10017

and by Routledge
2 Park Square, Milton Park, Abingdon, Oxon, OX14 4RN

*Routledge is an imprint of the Taylor & Francis Group, an informa business*

*Library of Congress Cataloging in Publication Data*
Goodman, Kenneth S.
    Reading—the grand illusion: how and why people make sense of print /
by Ken Goodman, Peter H. Fries, Steven L. Strauss.
    pages cm
    Includes bibliographical references.
    1. Reading. 2. Language and education.
    I. Fries, Peter Howard. II. Title.
    LB1573.G574 2016
    428.4–dc23
    2015027171

ISBN 978-1-138-99928-2 (hbk)
ISBN 978-1-138-99929-9 (pbk)
ISBN 978-1-315-65842-1 (ebk)

Typeset in Dante and Avenir
by Florence Production Ltd, Stoodleigh, Devon, UK

Printed and bound in the United States of America by
Edwards Brothers Malloy on sustainably sourced paper

This work is dedicated to all those who have searched for the reality of literacy so that we may provide the knowledge we gain to teachers and with them use that knowledge for universal literacy. Specifically it is dedicated to Edmund Huey who challenged us over a century ago to produce a comprehensive understanding of literacy.

No subject has been more studied and few aspects of reality have been more politicized or obfuscated than reading. So we also dedicate this work to the courage of those who came before us and those who will follow after us in persevering in the pursuit of knowledge no matter the risks.

Einstein said: "There is no logical way to the discovery of these elemental laws. There is only the way of intuition, which is helped by a feeling for the order lying behind the appearance."

*This life's five windows of the soul*
*Distorts the Heavens from pole to pole,*
*And leads you to believe a lie*
*When you see with, not thro', the eye.*

From *The Everlasting Gospel* (William Blake 1810)

# Brief Contents

# Contents

# Foreword

*Brian Cambourne*

**Game Changer**: *noun;* an event, idea, or procedure that effects a significant shift in the current way of doing or thinking about something.
*Example*: "This result is a potential game changer that could revitalize the entire US aerospace industry."

This book is a game changer. Not only can it *effect a significant shift in the current way of doing or thinking about* the teaching of reading, it also has the potential for *revitalizing the entire* reading education profession, from how we define effective reading behavior to how we do research, to how we teach reading.

This should not be interpreted as the typical hyperbolic embellishment found on blurbs or advertising materials used to promote books. I intend it to be a statement of fact. I truly believe that the format, content, and structure of this book is so dramatically different from the traditional genre of books about reading research and theory building that it has the potential to bring about a Kuhnian revolution in reading research and theory development on a number of levels.

This is an ambitious prediction. What makes this book so *dramatically different from the traditional genre of books about reading research and theory building?* The short answer is that its format, structure, and content are significantly different from the format, structure, and content of previous books which have attempted to present, explain, and justify particular theories of reading. Instead of tediously presenting research findings and interpreting what they *mean* for reading educators, this book leads its readers on a journey which subtly *persuades* them to explore and examine their own and others' reading behavior in ways that induce deeper understandings of the complexity of human symbolic behavior in general and the act of reading in particular.

How? What specific aspects of format, structure, or content make this possible? I identified four which I believe are critical for developing the narrative about *reading* and *learning to read* that the authors want their readers to construct.

Let me explain what they are.

One is the rejection of the long-standing tradition of *silo-isation* that has dominated the reading education profession for as long as I can remember. By *silo-isation* I mean the tendency of groups of specialists within complex domains of inquiry or knowledge to promote their own specialism as *the answer* to the ills of their profession or even of wider society. *Silo-isation* entails the slicing of complex knowledge domains (such as reading and reading education) along lines of specialization. This in turn creates *knowledge silos* which comprise clusters of like-minded scientists and thinkers sharing a common cause. Those who inhabit these silos believe that dividing experience and phenomena into increasingly smaller parts enhances understanding of the complex whole. Thus we have reading researchers who study **only** phonemic awareness, or word recognition, or readability and text complexity, or comprehension, and so on. These researchers obviously expect that by putting all these *slices* of the whole together again, either conceptually or experimentally, the whole system will become intelligible. The current chaotic state of reading education shows that this is a fallacy of the first order. The reading profession's tradition of breaking the complex act of reading and learning to read into parts and studying these parts has **not** improved its understanding of the complex system as a whole. Nor can it ever hope to, because reductionism not only distorts the system, it eventually destroys it.

The authors of this book obviously believe that the ever increasing confusion which *silo-isation* has created around reading research and theory building can only be eliminated by *boundary-crossing* scientists who are prepared to cross conventional borders of scientific concern in order to address the same problem. This is what the contributors to this book have done. The *common problem* is to construct, describe, and validate theory of *how reading works, how people make sense of print* by viewing it from the vantage of three different theoretical viewpoints. While Goodman views it through the lenses of teacher education and psycholinguistics, Fries views it through the perspective of modern linguistic science, bringing his expertise in structural, transformational, and systemic linguistics to the task. Strauss complements Fries' perspective by considering the problem from the dual perspectives of neurology and theoretical linguistics. A fourth perspective from the work of Eric Paulson adds studies of eye movements during reading to the perspectives of the three authors.

A second specific aspect of the format, structure, and content of this book is the decision to locate *reading* as a sub-category of the broader domain of human symbolic behavior. This subtly alerts readers to the possibility of an evolutionary basis for reading and learning to read, which in turn lays the groundwork for the preferred pedagogy of reading which is described later in the book. The possible connection to evolution is further reinforced by a title and sub-title which frames reading as a grand illusion, and then implies that it's an illusion which critically distorts the perception of what effective readers need to know and do in order to learn to read. By suggesting that illusions are both natural and necessary perceptual processes the brain uses to make sense of the world the authors invoke the possibility that, from an evolutionary perspective, accurate perception often has to be sacrificed in order to make a quick decision about what conditions in the environment *mean*.

The third crucial feature of the book's format, structure, and content is to identify the grand illusion which distorts the perception of how humans read alphabetic based scripts as the *common sense* belief that "reading involves the accurate, sequential recognition of words and that accurate word recognition is necessary for comprehension." Because this is a widely held assumption (i.e., it's a form of common sense) most reading educators will be aware of the implications it has for the pedagogy of reading. More importantly it provides a tighter, narrower focus for gradually unpacking the complexities of reading and learning to read in ways that "induce deeper understandings of the complexity of human symbolic behavior in general and the act of reading in particular."

The fourth and final feature, which sets the book apart from its predecessors, is the way it leads readers through these complexities by gently nudging them to construct a viable, cohesive theory that both explains the phenomena of reading and provides a basis for an evidence-based, scientifically-derived pedagogy for teaching reading. The authors do this by seamlessly embedding opportunities for readers to participate in mini-workshops and discuss some key results of the enormous repository of naturalistic research of "real kids reading real books" which Goodman and his colleagues and graduate students have completed over the last four decades. The contributions of Goodman, Fries, Strauss and Paulson are carefully woven through the text, and clearly illustrate how their different theoretical perspectives converge toward a cohesive explanatory theory of "how reading works, how people make sense of print."

Some of the most compelling scientific work of the twenty-first century has been done by researchers who seek inspiration and partnerships across disciplines and national borders. In the last decade such diverse experts as mechanical engineers, chemists, and evolutionary biologists have cooperated to design new enzymes for medical and energy research. Then there's an expert in human grammar who draws on expertise from computer science, anthropology, and neuroscience to inform his inquiries.

I'm hopeful that this book will mark the beginning of a movement to rework reading and learning to read using the tools and perspectives from a wide range of more successful scientific disciplines.

This book is not likely to nudge the entrenched researchers from their comfortable research silos. But it may stimulate a new generation of researchers to accept the book's challenge to study literacy as meaning making and to marvel at the universal ability of humans to think symbolically and to learn and create language easily in all its complex forms. And together, with informed teachers who come to understand that all children are capable of becoming literate as easily as they learned to talk, they can build exciting and effective pedagogy based on the understanding of literacy shared in this book.

Wollongong, Australia
August 2015

# Preface

## Sense and Common Sense

What is reading? Some researchers say it is just what common sense tells us it is. Look at the page. Start at the beginning. Look at the first word. Proceed left to right and top to bottom until you have identified each word on the page in the order in which the text presents them. Then turn the page and do it all over again.

And why does common sense tell us that that's what a reader does? First of all, it just feels that we do that—it's a strong gut feeling. Second, how else could we get the author's intended meaning if we don't identify the words as the author presented them? And third, if you simply listen to a reader read a page aloud, you will indeed hear the first word followed by the second followed by the third—until the last word is reached—more or less.

And common sense tells us one more thing—that the *identification* of each word on the page one after the next proceeds by *looking* at each word, one after the next.

Common sense? Maybe. But *not* what the scientific study of reading reveals to us. In fact, far from it. Because we have learned that readers who understand what they've read will say words that are indeed on the page without ever looking at them, say words that are not on the page and which they therefore could never have looked at, and not say words that they in fact have looked at. The most common belief about reading: that we identify every word in order as we read is an illusion. That's not what happens, yet we think it is.

Some researchers have devoted their careers to what they call a simple view of reading. They think that if they can find a few tests that correlate well with reading comprehension that by teaching to those tests children will be taught to read.

In this book we'll show that there is nothing simple about reading. Reading is one aspect of language that is really quite complex. Fortunately, language, including written language, is something we humans are really good at learning.

The purpose of this book is to explain not only what reading really is, but why common sense makes it seem to be something quite different from that reality. In other words, we will explain this *grand illusion*. And, as we shall see, unraveling the secrets of the grand illusion of reading will teach us about far more than reading itself. We will learn about how remarkable human language is. It will help us understand how the brain uses language, visually, to navigate the world. It will teach us about what it means to be human.

This book is written from three vantage points with a single perspective. The authors share a common view of how reading works, how people make sense of print. We've chosen to keep our separate voices rather than attempt to speak with one voice in order to give depth to our presentation. In this book we take on a formidable misconception: that reading involves the accurate, sequential recognition of words and that accurate word recognition is necessary for comprehension. We hope as you read the book you will come to see reading as the dynamic meaning-making process that it is.

## The Authors

**Ken Goodman** is in his sixth decade of studying the reading process as it happens in a wide range of real readers reading real texts. He's a teacher educator and a theoretician as well as a researcher. He developed miscue analysis as a way of getting at the process of reading by analyzing the unexpected things readers do as they read. That opens a window into what goes on in the reader's mind as meaning is constructed. We build here on a large body of miscue analysis research. Ken has developed a comprehensive model of how people make sense of written language. That comprehensive model is what we all share and what we hope to make available in this book.

**Peter H. Fries** is a second-generation linguist who rather uniquely represents the modern history of linguistics—the scientific study of language. Peter's father, Charles Fries, was a major descriptive linguist of the first half of the twentieth century. Peter was a student of Zellig Harris at the University of Pennsylvania a short time after Noam Chomsky studied with

Harris. And in recent decades Peter has been associated with systemic functional linguistics and Michael Halliday (1985), its chief architect. Peter is going to help us understand the grand illusion in reading from the linguist's perspective. Since reading is a language process, to understand it we need to view it as a linguist does.

**Steven L. Strauss** got his doctorate in linguistics from the Graduate Center at the City University, New York, and taught linguistics at the University of New Mexico. He then went to medical school and ultimately became a practicing neurologist. As a linguist and neurologist, Steve sees language when it is stressed in his patients and also brings the analytic skills of the professional linguist to this book. It was Steve who first realized the role of illusion in reading. To understand the grand illusion in reading, Steve is going to help us understand how the brain makes sense of language and of the world.

## Our Goal

Over several years the three of us have had some stimulating discussions. We've found our dialogs so informative that we decided to frame this book as dialogs among the authors. We have tried to reach a wide audience so we avoid use of too many scientific or technical terms and academic jargon. However we are dealing with complex, often counter-intuitive concepts. Rather than include a glossary, we define terms as we use them through examples and brief discussions of their meanings.

We hope that you, our readers, will see, as we have come to see, that:

- what readers do to make sense of print must be consistent with what they do in using any form of language;
- what goes on in the brain during reading has to be consistent with our understanding of how the brain does anything; and
- how the brain uses the eyes in reading must be consistent with how the brain uses the senses as tools for existing and functioning in the physical and social world.

Our goal of achieving comprehensive understanding of reading requires the perspectives we three represent. For clarity we'll precede each section with a picture of the writer.

# Acknowledgments

No book is an entity in and of itself. It is the product of its authors but it is built on the insights of many others who came before who have been concerned about the issues the book addresses. The book is a culmination of our life's work; it is at once a response to Edmund Huey's century old challenge that if we understood reading we would understand much of how the human brain works and at the same time a presentation of a comprehensive theory of how our species makes sense of written language.

We draw heavily on the work of: Edmund Huey, Frank Smith, Brian Cambourne, Margaret Meek Spencer, Louise Rosenblatt, Michael Halliday, Noam Chomsky, Jean Piaget, John Dewey, E. Brooks Smith, Harold Rosen, and James Britain.

Many people have been kind enough to read and respond to the manuscript in various stages.

Colleagues who collaborated in work represented in the book include Lois Bridges, Suzanne Gespass, Desmond Ryan, Alan Flurkey, Debra Goodman, Jassem Al-Fahid and Fred Gollasch.

Special acknowledgment to Eric Paulson for his eye movement and EMMA research which is central to the main theses of this book.

Yetta Goodman has contributed in too many ways to completely acknowledge. Likewise Nancy Fries has been present at all stages of the work.

Thanks to Marie Ruiz and Kelly Allen for their hard work and diligence in bringing the manuscript into final shape. And thanks to Naomi Silverman for her encouragement and guidance.

**Ken Goodman\*, Peter H. Fries,**
**and Steven L. Strauss**

---

\* This book is presented as a dialogue among the authors with each author writing the sections and side bars that follow their pictures. I have edited the manuscript during the making of the book for which I take full responsibility.

# Illusions: What We See and What We Perceive 1

 Language in all its varieties and forms is the most unique characteristic of all that defines our species. Of all creatures we alone have the ability to connect with others of our species so completely that we can communicate our most intimate feelings and thoughts, share in the experience of others vicariously, and reason in complex ways—and all this is possible because we have language. Furthermore each of us individually and collectively has the ability to create or invent language and modify it to serve our changing personal and social needs.

## Language: Our Most Human Characteristic

No parent can help but be delighted and amazed at the universal ability of infants to begin to speak and understand the language or languages around them. They accomplish this at such a tender age that some scholars have come to believe that language isn't learned, but rather is innate. We believe that what is innate in our single human species is the ability to think symbolically and create language.

Language, we believe, is a personal and social invention. Three human characteristics make language possible: first, we are social beings who cannot survive or live a full life without complex connections to each other. And second, we think symbolically: that is, we let complex abstract systems of sounds, scribbles, or motions represent our meanings. And, of course, we are an intelligent species. What would be the point of having language if we didn't have things to say to each other?

Language is so marvelous that it leads to two rather opposite common views. One is that language is just there. We all come to use at least one of its many varieties without much thought about how or why this happens. The other is that language is itself an inscrutable mystery. And it is true no one theory or system has yet been produced by linguists that can fully describe or account for all aspects of even a single language.

## Reading Is Language

This book is about reading. And because reading is a language process it is also about language. Since our species has the ability to invent new forms of language as our need and ability to connect with each other expands, both individuals and societies usually begin with oral language. Oral language serves the purposes of face-to-face communication. It is spoken and heard. As our need to connect becomes more complex—when we need to connect over time and/or space—written language is developed. For most hearing people, oral language is the first form of language to develop. But the ability to create language is not limited to speech. Deaf people can connect through manual signs and blind people can read through touch.

Our human need to connect is so strong that we have extended both oral and written language through digital technology. Oral language can be broadcast over distance and preserved over time so it overlaps the functions of written language. And digital writing on computers and cell phones can provide instantaneous dialog. Language multiplies human intelligence as we can think together and build on each other's insights. Stored language expands human memory and the reach of our voices over great distances and over time. It connects us and fills our libraries and now our cyberspace. Truly, technology has made it possible to put the wisdom of the ages at the fingertips of each of us, all represented in language. Our ability to use symbolic representation is not confined to language. We assign significance to objects, numbers, dates, colors—almost anything. And we can express emotions and concepts through music, art, and dance.

Once we are comfortable users of a language we have the sense of dealing directly with meaning with little conscious thought, most of the time, to how we are accomplishing that. In this book we intend to make you aware of what you are actually doing as you make sense of written language. Reading is not inscrutable. But it is indeed marvelous. Some common-sense beliefs about how reading works are untrue, as is often the case of the things we do so often without thinking about how we do what we do.

## The Illusion of Reading Every Word

We will help you understand that one such popular belief is that when you read you are recognizing the words on the page from left to right as they are printed.

It is likly that you think your seeing every word now as you reed this book. You you may find it hard to except the idea that you could of missed noticing some vary obvious typos. A side from that, the idea that accurate reading is an illusion maybe strange considering most of us were taught that accurate reading is necessary four comprehension.

To understand how we make sense of print you need to understand that the idea that you read every word is an illusion. We call it a "grand illusion" because it is so important in understanding what reading is and how it is learned and taught. You may have thought you saw a misprint in the paragraph above. Now please go back over that paragraph and count the number of errors we deliberately put there. How many did you find? None? 2? 6? 12? How many were there?

Have we teased you to find out how and why this happens? The grand illusion in reading is no clever magician's trick. It goes to the heart of how our brains work to make sense not only of reading but of the world as we find our way around it.

### Edmund Huey's Challenge

In 1908 Edmund Huey wrote:

> so to completely analyze what we do when we read would almost be the acme of a psychologist's achievements, for it would be to describe very many of the most intricate workings of the human mind, as well as to unravel the tangled story of the most remarkable specific performance that civilization has learned in all its history.
>
> (p. 6)

We dedicate this book to Edmund Huey as we share what we have learned about reading and the "most intricate workings of the human mind."

## Limitations of Our Senses and Illusions of the Human Brain

 Illusions permeate our everyday mental life. Of course, we are not always aware of the illusion we are experiencing. In fact, the vast majority of illusions go undetected. Still, a natural curiosity takes over; we often feel satisfied only if we make sense of the illusion, and we may be bothered by failing to understand it. Why did I think one thing when the reality was something else altogether?

This dilemma is precisely the key to understanding illusions. The very fact that illusions exist, that they generally go undetected, reveals how the brain's various psychological mechanisms work collaboratively to make sense of the world. In doing so, accurate perception may be sacrificed for the preferred sensation of having made sense.

### Illusions Arise from Distinct Sources

Countless illusions are rooted in the simple biological fact that our sensory organs—those collections of cells that allow us to detect light and color and sound and physical texture—are far less complete in their detail than the world they are trying to detect. Human eyes can only detect light within a certain range of wave length. They do not have the resolution capacity of pit vipers in detecting infrared, for example. The ears can only detect sounds within a certain frequency range. They do not have the resolution capacity of our canine companions. We certainly lack dogs' acute sense of smell. As the renowned neurologist V.S. Ramachandran (2004) has stated: "We need to construct useful, virtual reality simulations of the world that we can act on" (Ramachandran, 2004: 105). In other words we use our incomplete sensory information to construct an illusory world that is (usually) sufficiently accurate that we can act on it.

### The Blind Spot Illusion

The eye contains layers of nerve cells that detect electromagnetic radiation that corresponds to the colors of the spectrum. These retinal cells line the back of the eye, each one sending along the visual information it has detected to a central meeting point also in the back of the eye. Imagine photodetectors

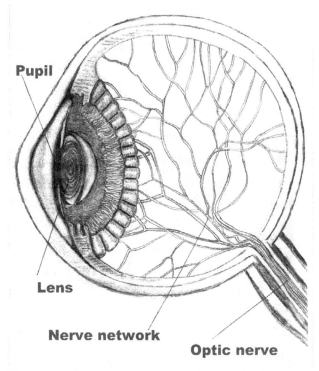

**Figure 1.1** The Human Eye. Original art by Shoshana Pearson

completely covering the surface of a wall, each with a long wire headed toward a hole in the middle of the wall, with all the wires meeting at that hole and diving into it to deliver their information to the next relay station.

Only one spot on the wall contains no photoreceptor, and that is the spot where the hole is. For the retina, a similar hole exists where the nerve wires meet as they continue their journey all together to the next relay station in the brain. Therefore, any light that lands only on the area of the hole goes undetected. The visual picture created by the merging together of the retinal information contains a blind spot right in the middle of the visual field. Sophisticated studies have demonstrated that the brain "fills in" the blind spot.

That is worth emphasizing—the brain, not the eye itself, fills in the blind spot. And it fills it in such a way that there appears to be a seamless continuity between that part of the visual picture constructed from actual electromagnetic input and that part projected onto the picture by the brain itself. Therefore, what we perceive is the illusion of a scene determined entirely by the world outside us, by what we are looking at. In truth, a piece of that scene was patched in by the brain.

There is a functional advantage in the construction of a visual scene that makes sense because of its consistency, as opposed to one that does not make sense because we don't really believe that the person we are looking at has a hole in his forehead.

## Away From and Toward Reality

Sometimes illusions move away from objective reality as you did when you read and missed some of the errors in the paragraph on page 3. The blind spot illusion abstracts *toward* reality, and creates a perceptual visual scene that is actually a truer representation of the objective world.

But despite the quite opposite character of these illusions, they are united in a common feature: they construct mental representations that make sense within a specific context and that permit efficient and effective transactions within that context.

Illusion, in other words, is created in the normal and natural course of the brain's transaction with the world and the limitations of our sensory equipment to accurately represent it. What matters, though, is not the degree of accuracy of the sensory equipment, but rather that the brain can make sense of the sensory information detected, however limited or distorted it may be.

As we have just observed, perception is only partly accurate. Many true aspects of the objective world are detected, but most are ignored. Experienced drivers can focus on the small red or green light in an intersection that tells them to stop or go and ignore all the other lights and signs. We even distort those aspects we do detect, as when we perceive a uniform shade of green in a landscape with many different shades of green. We believe that we have perceived accurately, even when we haven't. One role of science is to investigate the mismatches between the real world and what we have come to believe about it both individually and socially.

## Accurate Perception Is an Illusion

Even more intriguing is that what creates the illusion of accurate perception is having made sense of the visual, auditory, or tactile scene. When making sense fails, we simultaneously conclude that what we thought was an accurate perception of the world was in fact quite inaccurate. We do not, of course, rest at the realization of inaccuracy in our perception. We take the new information and construct a new interpretation, one that now makes better sense. That's what we will demonstrate happens in reading. That's what happens in life.

But, you might ask, haven't we just admitted that even though we thought we did, we didn't really make sense of the scene? This is a very important question. For it is quite true that just because we think we have made sense, our hypothetical little mini-theory of a visual scene may turn out to have been wrong. Or we may have used faulty logic in making sense without realizing it. Or we may have used a false premise in our sense-making reasoning. For any number of reasons, the sense we construct may, in fact, be nonsense or incomplete. Just because we believe we have made sense does not mean that this is always the case. The sense we make depends on prior knowledge (what we knew before).

There is a dynamic interaction among these three components of interpreting the world—perception, sense, and belief. The interaction between these components is hierarchical. Making sense trumps being accurate and believing that we have made sense trumps whether we have truly made sense. Consider the conflicting accounts of multiple witnesses to the same accident or crime.

## On Seeing and Knowing

Steve's discussion raises some important issues about the relationship between seeing and knowing.

Consider this well-known illusion:

Every morning, as long as our species has been on the Earth, we have looked to the east and seen the sun rise, move across the sky and dependably set in the west. We *know* the sun is there, moving across the sky, even if it is obscured by clouds from our view. And for many centuries the few people who suggested an alternative explanation were ridiculed and in extreme cases treated quite badly, such as being burned at the stake as heretics.

Sometimes—indeed too often—illusions are so strongly believed to be real that scientific understandings of reality are rejected. When Galileo, the world's leading scientist in the seventeenth century (Sobel, 1999), looked at Jupiter through a recent invention, the telescope, and saw what he concluded were moons circling it, he knew that what appeared to be the movement of the sun around the Earth was an illusion that resulted from the spinning in space of the Earth as it moved in orbit around the sun. Yet he risked his life and liberty by revealing the truth. We can call this illusion that the Earth was the center of the solar system a grand illusion because it was so widely believed that it had become an important part of church dogma. Copernicus (Sobel, 2011) waited until he was dying before he took the risk of saying that this was an illusion.

Consider another illusion:

For many centuries, with our vantage points tied by gravity to the Earth's surface, only a few navigators suspected that we were all standing on a huge sphere. Before there was proof that the world was a rough sphere, the idea that we wouldn't fall off when we reached its edges was too complex for most people to accept—even those who sailed with Columbus. And when Copernicus explained night and day, saying the Earth spins on its axis, that was beyond belief for most people. Surely we would fly off the Earth if it were spinning!

## Is Seeing Believing?

Some scientists are fond of saying "I only know what I see." But if that were so, our understanding of the relationship between seeing and knowing would be severely limited. And we surely know a lot about things we can't see. We commonly use the word "see" with several different meanings.

See, as in "I see you" when playing peekaboo with a small child. In other words: you are visible to me.

See, as in "Sometimes when I look at the tiles on the floor, I see one pattern and then suddenly I see a whole different pattern." Since the visual input hasn't changed, what changes must be how the brain organizes that input. A synonym for that *see* would be *perceive*. What the brain makes of what we see is what we perceive. And many illusions seem to be tricks our brains play on us. Or perhaps not tricks at all but necessary adjustments the brain makes to make sense of what the eye sees.

See, as in "I didn't get it before but now I see what you mean." This see means understand.

Other meanings of see include:

- "See you later."
- "She's been seeing Bob lately."
- "I'll see you and raise you 20."

There is a difference between seeing and perceiving and a difference between perceiving and knowing. So some scientists say: "No, you don't know what you see. You see what you know."

## Making Sense

Steve has shown us that the brain is where we make sense of the world. From the time we're born we build the world—in our heads. Jean Piaget calls that *psychogenesis* (Piaget, 1979). We discover that objects have permanence even when we don't see them. We learn to judge distances and directions and how our world is organized. We're comforted when things happen the way we expect them to—and we're agitated when they don't. Our brains are constantly learning and they use what they know to transact with the world. We do this in our heads but also in the context of our interactions with our families, our friends, and our neighbors as we transact with the people around us. As we grow into a society and a culture, we learn to see things as our family and neighbors see them. The virtual world we invent comes into harmony with the world of our cultures and our communities.

Philosophers are roughly divided between realists and idealists. Realists start from the premise that there is a real world which we come to know. Idealists start from the premise that all we know is what our brains construct. But both agree that when we *see* something our brains turn it into a **perception**. What we **think we see** is more important than what **we actually see**. We make it fit what we know and how we've come to see in order to understand the world. Piaget calls that *assimilation*. When a thing doesn't fit, we either ignore what **we see** because we don't understand it or we reinterpret it. We literally change it to make it fit. Or we change ourselves. Piaget says we accommodate and change how we organize our world to see the reality we hadn't seen before (Piaget, 1971).

So what is an illusion and what is the truth? If what we "know" is verified as we transact with our world, we believe it to be true and continue to act on it. If some experience causes us to lose confidence in our self-constructed reality, we reconstruct it. All our understandings of the world are built in this way. We always have to be ready to revise our view of the reality around us.

All animals have brains. Ours has some special features that give us the ability to think symbolically. We can let abstractions represent not only things but ideas, relationships, and even our complex schemas. And so that makes it possible for us to create and use language. With language we can share how we see (perceive) things and what we learn with others. We not only form perceptions from what we see but our brain uses what it knows and how it organizes it to predict what it will experience: when a traffic light will change, when a ball hit from a bat will reach a certain point so it can be caught, which way the door knob will turn and how it will feel if it is locked or unlocked. The brain tells the eye what it expects and sends it to look for certain information it needs.

## Perceptual Illusions

Some illusions are at the level of perceptions. What we think we see is not what is actually there. The full moon in the photo below seems to be extraordinarily large as it rises above the horizon, much larger than it would look later when it moves higher in the sky. The common explanation is that the moon appears to us to be bigger as it rises because the light is spread as it passes through the thick atmosphere. I am grateful to physicist Charles Buchanan for correcting this misconception:

> Despite protestations to the contrary, double-exposure photographs prove that the physical image size of the moon is the same when it is

**Figure 1.2** The Full Moon.

Photo: Stefan Seip (www.astromeeting.de)

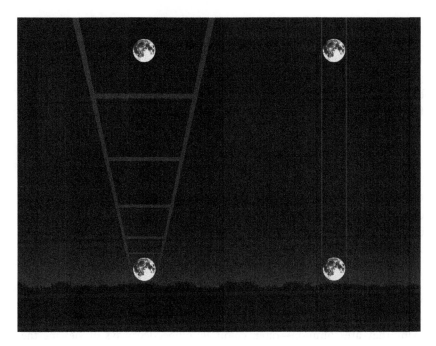

**Figure 1.3** True Moon Illusion
© Gary A. Becker, astronomy.org © 2015. Used with permission.

overhead as when it is on the horizon. A perceptual illusion is created in our mind/brain by the presence of Earthly "reference" objects (trees, etc.) on the horizon that the moon's image is larger when it is on the horizon than when it is overhead. There is a very tiny actual physical difference due to the density differences in the atmosphere near the Earth. But this is so small that it is not detectable, as substantiated by the photographs.

(personal communication, September, 2014)

Magicians have examined the way the brain organizes visual input into perceptions and much of their magic is based on this knowledge. A coin in one hand of the magician is "seen" by an audience being thrown to the other hand. But it has disappeared. Actually it never left the first hand. An illusion of the brain created a transfer that never actually took place.

Our brains must construct models of the world and use our senses to cope with the real world. The eye depends on its lens to provide the brain, indirectly, with clear images. But it can only do that when it stops and fixates. So our sense that we see a world in motion is an illusion, but an important one—the brain knows the world doesn't lurch from stop to stop like the eye does. It fills in what it has learned and we perceive the world in motion. That's why we're certain that we saw the coin move from hand to hand. The "moving picture" doesn't move. It is a series of still pictures moving so fast that the brain reconstructs the motion that was recorded. Both the magician and the film industry take advantage of the perceptual illusions the brain depends on.

## Conceptual Illusions

Other illusions are at the conceptual level. Often, but not always, they are based on some interpretation or misinterpretation of what we think we see. The illusion of the sun moving across the sky was the basis for the misconception that the Earth was the center of the universe.

Misconceptions are formed in much the same way as valid conceptions. The brain constructs a concept from its experiences within a social context. Who is a friend and who is a stranger—or even an enemy? Sometimes we call widely held misconceptions "common sense" because they are believed by so many they are common—often culturally embedded ways of viewing the world. Most of science involves going beyond common sense to carefully examine these beliefs and find ways of getting closer to what is real. Misconceptions are deeply imbedded and often very hard to change. At their worst they become prejudices or stereotypes.

## Sense and Accuracy

With my students and associates, we studied oral reading of hundreds of different readers in a number of languages and at all levels of proficiency. We found that readers are, and should be, much more concerned with making sense than getting each word right. I named this research *miscue analysis* (Goodman, 1969) and it led to the socio-psycholinguistic model of reading the authors share (see Chapter 4).

In miscue analysis the reader is asked to read an entire text aloud. This is recorded and a typescript of the story is marked showing every place where what the reader says (the observed response (OR) differs from what was expected (ER)) the miscues. Systematically comparing the oral reading responses with the expected responses provides a window into the head of the reader. Every reader in our studies, who read a page or more, made some miscues. Proficient readers who understand what they are reading omit, insert, substitute, and otherwise revise the text as they read. They construct their own internal texts alongside that of the author. Often they correct themselves when they have lost the sense of what they are reading. Making sense does not require an exact, accurate reproduction of the author's text. In fact, preoccupation with accuracy can often distract the reader from the meaning. And accuracy requires extraordinary effort which would be inefficient for most purposes other than a performance such as choral reading or news casting.

A proficient reader is likely to believe that what he or she reads is a verbatim rendition of the author's text, even when audio recordings attest to the contrary. That's a powerful illusion.

Eric Paulson (2000) added studies of eye movements during reading to our oral reading miscue studies. Now we are not only able to compare what the reader reads out loud with what we expect from the text, but we also have the record of what the eyes are doing during the reading: where the eye stops (fixates), how long it lingers there, and when it sweeps from fixation to fixation.

On page 3 we included a paragraph that contained a number of errors. Below is the same paragraph with the 11 errors numbered and corrected:

**Table 1.1** Errors Numbered and Corrected

It is (1) _likely_ that you think (2) <u>you're</u> seeing every word now as you (3) <u>read</u> this book. You (4) <u>you</u> may find it hard to (5) <u>accept</u> the idea that you (6) <u>could've</u> missed noticing some (7) <u>very</u> (8) <u>obvious</u> typos. (9) <u>Aside</u> from that, the idea that accurate reading is an illusion (10) <u>may be</u> strange considering most of us were taught that accurate reading is necessary (11) <u>for</u> comprehension.

# References

Goodman, K. S. (1969). "Analysis of oral reading miscues: Applied psycholinguistics." *Reading Research Quarterly*, 5(1), 9–30.

Halliday, M. A. K. (1985). *An introduction to functional grammar*. London: E. Arnold.

Huey, E. B. (1908/1968). *The psychology and pedagogy of reading*. Cambridge, MA: MIT Press.

Paulson, E. (2000). *Adult readers' eye movements during the production of oral miscues*. The University of Arizona, (Doctoral dissertation). Retrieved from ProQuest Dissertations and Theses database. (UMI No. 9972086)

Piaget, J. (1971). *Psychology and epistemology*. New York: Grossman.

Piaget, J. (1979). "La psychogènese des connaissances et sa signification épistémologique." In Piatelli-Palmarini, M. (Ed.), *Théories du langage, théories de l'apprentissage*. Paris: Seuil.

Ramachandran, V.S. (2004). *A brief tour of human consciousness*. New York: Pi Press.

Sobel, D. (1999). *Galileo's daughter: A historical memoir of science, faith, and love*. New York: Walker.

Sobel, D. (2011). *A more perfect heaven: How Copernicus revolutionized the cosmos*. London: Bloomsbury.

# The Grand Illusion in Reading    **2**

The common view of reading among both professionals and the public is an illusion so significant that we can justifiably call it the grand illusion in reading:

*We think we see every letter and every word as we read a text.*

We're calling this a grand illusion because it is, like the illusion of the Earth standing still while the sun, moon, and planets move around us, so evident but so wrong. But it is also a grand illusion because it dominates not only how readers in general think about reading, but also how prominent researchers and instructional authorities think about reading.

For many researchers, this grand illusion is so obvious that it does not need to be examined. Reading instruction has been focused on getting readers to attend carefully to the print, to examine the letters carefully—even in nonsense syllables—because it seems so clear that reading is seeing all the letters in order to recognize all the words. How else could we read?

Like all major illusions, what we believe we see as we read seems so obvious that we find it hard to consider any alternative. Yet this illusion is just as wrong as the illusion that the sun moves around the Earth. Even though you may have had trouble finding all of the embedded errors in the introduction, I hear you saying "I see all the letters in all the words right now as I'm reading." And that's more or less true. You can see each letter in each word when you concentrate on doing that. Or can you?

## Illusions and the Grand Illusion

It's fair that you are unconvinced that this is any kind of illusion. Therefore let's try a small experiment:

Get yourself a piece of paper and a pencil. Then read the short, one paragraph story in Figure 2.1. Read it through once—don't go back in your reading. When you have finished reading it, cover the story and write down everything you remember reading.

---

## The Boat in the Basement

A woman was building a boat in her

basement. When she had finished the

the boot, she discovered that it was

too big to go though the door. So he

had to take the boat a part to get

it out. She should of planned ahead.

(Gollasch adapted from Goodman, 1980)

---

**Figure 2.1** The Boat in the Basement

*DISCUSSION*

Let's look first at what you wrote. Here are some questions for you to think about before you look back at the story.

**Did you print or write in your usual handwriting?**

My instructions to you were to write down everything you remember reading. If you didn't write it in the printed form you read, that means that you didn't think my instructions meant that you should remember and reproduce what you saw, but rather what you remember of the content or meaning of the story. In fact, without looking back you will have a hard time remembering details of the font. So if you think you look at every letter in every word as you read, wouldn't you have been better able to remember what the print looked like? Which letter A did you see? What you wrote is most likely your usual a, probably cursive.

**Did you find yourself going back and rereading during the reading?**

I specifically told you not to go back but to read it through once and once only. Did you find yourself rereading to get more information because something in the story didn't quite fit? If you didn't regress in your reading, did you want to regress? If you did go back, did you feel guilty doing so? From both my experience with others reading this story and my theoretical understanding of how reading works, I can predict that most of you reading this story did regress—scanning back over the text because your

 Because the grand illusion caused optometrists and others to think that regressing was a bad habit which needed to be eliminated from reading, you may have been asked at some time to read a text produced by a tachistoscope. That's a machine that produces a text that disappears after you read it. This was used to teach people not to regress.

brain needed more input—even though I told you not to go back. That must mean that you weren't sure what you saw and you needed to take another look to make sense of the story. Now again, don't look back yet at the paragraph in answering this next question.

**Did you notice any errors or typos as you read the story?**

If, as you read, there were typos in the text, shouldn't you have "seen" all of them? If you see all the letters of all the words as you read, you would certainly have noticed all the typos in this story. Look at what you wrote. Did you write anything differently because you thought there was an error in the text?

I'll call your attention now to one error in the text which you probably did notice. It's likely that you perceived that the word *boot* appeared where you expected *boat*. In fact, I deliberately chose a font here where the a and the o are very close in appearance. That means you noticed a very slight difference in appearance because it didn't seem to fit your expectation.

In the paragraph above I use the word *perceived* because it's what your brain did with what you saw that would cause you to think it was a typo. Otherwise you would not have rejected *boot* as not fitting the text. That must mean that you have certain expectations or predictions as you make sense of the text so you are more likely to notice things which don't fit your predictions.

Now consider what other "typos" you did or didn't notice. Jot them down and we'll discuss them a little later. In fact, now I'm going to ask you to go back and carefully reread the story and this time look specifically for errors. List them all in the order you find them.

How many did you find this time with careful rereading? I'll tell you now that there are actually six errors deliberately embedded in the story. Have you found them all yet? We've used this story with many groups and it's been used in several research studies so I have strong data on which embedded errors are more and less likely to be found.

Some of you were so sure you would see all the words and the letters in them that you didn't "play the game." You looked carefully at every word— yet it is very unlikely, even if you did that, that you were aware of more than three or four of the six embedded errors. There is actually an extra word in the story that turns out to be the hardest of all the embedded errors to find. Did you find it yet? Look at the end of the second line and the beginning of the third line. Aha! How is it possible that almost everyone who reads this story does not see the two *the's*? Actually we'll provide you with evidence later that you most likely did see both *the*'s but your brain did not perceive them. The eye sends the signal to the brain but the brain rejects it. If reading is making sense of a written text rather than paying close attention to the letters and the words then it must be that the brain ignores the extra word because it already has the sense and the grammar of English that it can't permit two *the*'s in a row in that sentence.

Let's look now at what you wrote. Did you use the word *through* in your writing? Look at line four in the story. Does it say *through*? No, it says *though*. So why is it unlikely that you would notice the missing letter?

One thing I can assure you is that it wasn't carelessness on your part. Not likely, when so many readers fail to "notice" the error. What does your brain know that would cause you to overlook this error? You have learned through your reading that those -ough words are undependable. Your brain is selective about which information it needs to make sense of a written passage: it perceives what it expects to see. If it doesn't, then it tells the eye to go back and check for more information. Also your knowledge about language tells you that you need a preposition in that language slot so you consider an -*ough* word that is most likely to occur.

Here, for you to consider, are the other three embedded errors:

> *a part should be apart*
> *he should be she in line four of the story*
> *should of in the last line*

It should've been what? Not *should have* but *should've*. Because of the odd spelling of *of* this is a very common spelling error. Try the trick of asking friends to count the *f*s on a whole page of text. They'll undercount them every time. Did you know that almost no English spellings end in v? Printers add an *e* to words ending in that sound, as in "the dove dove through the window."

We have both informal data from the use of this story with many audiences and more formal data from our research studies. See how your experience fits with our data.

Whether seventh graders or college undergraduates, no one finds all the errors even with unlimited time on the second reading. The mean for all readers is something less than three errors detected with limited time. The order of difficulty (from most difficult to least): the two *the*'s, *though* rather than *through*, *should of*, *a part*, *he* for *she* and *boot* for *boat*.

I hope this exploration of reading this story with embedded errors has been interesting and fun. You may want to try it with family or friends to share the fun. But this little demonstration is not just a curiosity. Nor are there any tricks involved that make this text unique. I hope it is sufficient for us to agree that the common-sense belief that we see all the letters and words when we read is in fact an illusion.

Of course it is not enough to know that reading is not the sequential recognition of letters and words. We need now to understand why you had difficulty detecting the errors. It would be so simple to say it's because reading is not recognizing words and how they are spelled but rather making sense of print. But we need to understand not just that this happens but why and how it works this way. How do you read if it isn't recognizing letters and words and why didn't you see all those errors?

## Vision and Perception in Reading: Learning about Reading with EMMA*

* This section is contributed by Eric Paulson

In order to understand how reading works we need to understand what the eyes are doing as we read. Even just watching someone's eyes while they read the newspaper, or a book, or a blog can reveal a lot about what happens "behind the scenes" in reading. In fact, what is widely considered the first eye movement research study, by Emile Javal in 1879, did just that: he watched readers' eyes while reading.

Before getting to the admittedly more interesting aspects of what eye-movement research reveals about reading processes, it is important to first focus on some information about what the eyes are *not* able to do. Physiologically, the eyes have restrictions as a data source in reading, and we will focus on two of those boundaries here: that of what the eye can use while in motion, and the amount of text the eye can access.

First, the eye must stop and focus on text in order for that portion of text to be useful for the reader because the brain gets no usable information from the text while the eye is moving (Dodge, 1900; Rayner, 1997; Wolverton and Zola, 1983). These "stops" are termed *fixations*. The movement between fixations is called a *saccade*.

Second, only a little of the text is in clear focus during each fixation. The region of the eye which provides in-focus information is termed the fovea, and it subsumes only 1–2 degrees of visual angle (about 3–6 letter spaces) around the point of fixation (Just and Carpenter, 1987: 30). In terms of reading, this means that only the part of the text that the reader is directly fixating—about a word (or two, if the words are short)—is physiologically able to be accurately discerned by the reader. Letters that are viewed outside of that window are seen as gross shapes, but not as distinguishable, in-focus letters.

 It is interesting that the size of the font may influence how much information is in the area of sharp focus. And since Chinese characters convey more meaning in less space than spelled out words they would also provide more information in sharp focus to their readers.

Taken together, these two characteristics of the eye as a data source during reading mean that readers' eyes must pause in order to get useful information, and that during that pause they only get about a word-length of information in focus.

The physiological restrictions of the eye previously noted indicate that in order to see a word in focus, for the most part that word must be directly fixated. However, only about 2–3 to 3–4 of the words in a given text are looked at by readers (Fisher and Shebilske, 1985; Judd and Buswell, 1922; Just and Carpenter, 1987; Rayner, 1997). Thus, the first thing to understand about what eye movement research shows us about reading processes is that readers do not look at every word while reading.

 There are actual neurons going from the cortex of the brain to the thalamus that suppress background information from the eye as the brain concentrates on what is its main concern: meaning.

Additionally, the words that readers do look at are not necessarily looked at in the order they are presented in the text. That is, readers do not sample the text sequentially. About 10–20 percent of fixations are regressions (Rayner and Pollatsek, 1989), meaning readers' eyes proceed from right to left through a previously viewed section of text. The example below is from Paulson, Flurkey, Goodman, and Goodman (2003). In this excerpt from a reading of a general interest, expository magazine article, the reader looked at eight of the 14 words (57 percent) in the sentence, visually skipping several words. And the words that he directly looked at are not in sequential order: he looked at *the*, then *polenta*, then *the* again, then *cornmeal*, *often*, *beans*, then *beans* again, then onto *sausage*, back to *beans* and onto *sausage* and *floating* and back to *sausage*, before looking at *floating* twice, and then to *in*, the final word he looked at in the sentence.

While this reader read aloud "take polenta, the cornmeal mush often served with beans and sausage floating in it," what he looked at while reading was the / polenta / the / cornmeal / often / beans / beans / sausage / beans / sausage / floating / sausage / floating / floating / in. So this reader looked

**Table 2.1** Regressive Eye Movements

Take polenta, the cornmeal mush
2  1 3       4

often served with beans and sausage floating in it.
5            6 7 9        8 12  10   11  14  13 15

Source: reprinted from Paulson, Flurkey, Goodman, and Goodman, 2003, p. 349.

at the text in an order that would seem to produce syntactic gibberish. However, he produced an oral text that is verbatim to the published text. Why? Here is where the illusion comes in, because reading involves a search for information, not simply a visual "grab" of all the letters. Eye movement research shows that readers regress—go backwards—10–20 percent of the time (Rayner and Pollatsek, 1989: 432). This isn't a regular, automatic motor activity on the part of the reader, it's an attempt to get more information, disconfirm a prediction, fix a misconception, and so on. Eye movement researcher Hogaboam (1983: 314–315) concludes that:

> Models assuming this [sequential word by word process] characteriza-
> tion of eye movements might be disregarding over three-fourths of the
> normal eye movement data . . . The point to be taken from this is that
> it is inaccurate to characterize skilled reading as a process of moving one's
> eyes forward from one word to the next with occasional regressions.

So this non-sequential eye movement pattern made during the production of sequential oral reading is common and an interesting aspect of reading being a non-sequential process of meaning-making. Readers selectively sample different parts of the text, based on their background knowledge, purpose for reading, and expectations of what they will find in the text, in order to inform the meaning-making process, a process that does not assume linearity as a necessary component of meaning-construction.

Combining eye movement analysis with other research tools can be very informative, and an example of such a fruitful combination is found in Eye Movement Miscue Analysis (EMMA) (Duckett, 2008; Kim, Knox, and Brown, 2007; Paulson, 2002), where a reader's visual eye movement data is combined with the reader's verbal miscues (places where the reader departs from the text when reading aloud) data to produce a powerful view into a reader's approach to reading a particular text. The following example (adapted from Paulson and Freeman, 2003) shows an excerpt from a short story; the reader's oral reading omissions—where he "skipped" a word while reading aloud—are marked with the miscue notation of a circle.

**Table 2.2** Omissions

---

All the doors are locked, right? And (all) the windows, ditto.

Okay, (then) So I feel like an idiot, trying to stay up all night.

---

**Table 2.3** Fixations

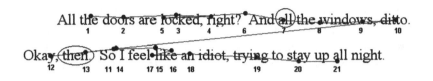

Source: reprinted from Paulson and Freeman, 2003: p.56.

The reader omitted two words in this excerpt while reading aloud: "all" and "then." Traditional understandings of the relationship between the eye and the voice would dictate that the reader probably skipped those words visually, opening the door for an oral reading miscue. That is not what happened, however. In Table 2.3, the same excerpt is provided, with the same reader's miscues noted. In addition, his fixations are now added to the picture.

Note that the two words the reader omitted were both fixated (see dots 7 and 13)—in contrast to traditional intuitions that we must not have looked at the words we unintentionally omit, this reader looked right at those two words that he did not read orally. Note also that there are several words that he did *not* look at (All, are, the, I, feel, idiot, to, up, night), but still read aloud. The reader fixated 60 percent of the words, and made two oral word omissions. Forty percent of the words were not looked at by the reader, including *All, are, to,* and *night,* and it would seem intuitive that these words would be among those verbally omitted. However, as the example demonstrates, the orally omitted words were not included in the 40 percent of the words which were visually skipped by the reader: the words he verbally omitted, *all* and *then,* were both directly fixated. The reader looked right at the words that he verbally omitted,

 We could consider that the reader is filling in omitted words mentally but this would miss the point. The reader is constructing his/her own text. If the words not fixated are included it is because the reader inferred they were there. In the same way fixated words may be miscued in that what the reader constructs makes sense without them. The reader is making sense and may be influenced by but is not limited in doing so by the particular word choices of the author. Miscues also result from the process of meaning construction. Reading which appears accurate also results from that same process.

and read aloud words he did not look at—perhaps a counter-intuitive phenomenon, but one that should not be unexpected if readers are actively constructing meaning instead of simply looking at the text and absorbing each word in the order it is presented. This is not just an isolated example, but has been shown to be a pattern; Paulson found that ". . . readers were as likely to fixate a word they orally substituted or omitted as they were to fixate a word they produced verbatim to the text" (2002: 62).

Eye movements clearly show the reader doing what is necessary in order to make sense of the text, including actively sampling the text and utilizing context as an important part of the reading process. Readers *construct* meaning with the text. In short, eye movement research provides support for viewing the reading process from a constructivist framework. Let's take an in-depth look at one reading of *The Boat in the Basement* that should help you understand why you didn't see all the embedded errors.

The following section deals with Evan, a teenager reading *The Boat in the Basement* while his eyes are being tracked is adapted from Paulson and Freeman (2003, pp. 19–21).

**Table 2.4** Eye Movements in Evan's 1st Reading

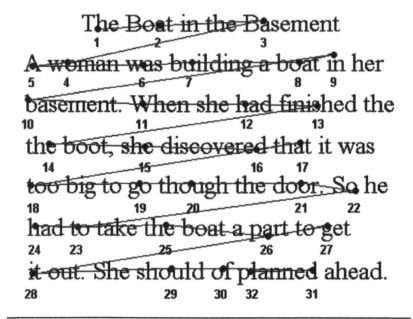

Evan was given the same instructions that we gave above—to read the paragraph one time through and write what he remembered reading. The points indicated where Evan looked the first time he read the paragraph.

Like other readers we've discussed, he fixated about 61 percent of the words in the text. If we take a close look at the errors that are in the text, we find that he fixated one of the *the's, though, part* (from *a part*), and *should of*. After reading it through one time, he wrote the following as his written retelling of the text:

*The Boat in the Basement*

A woman was building a boat in the basement. When she was through, she realized that it wouldn't fit through the door. The woman had to take it apart to fit it through the door. She should have planned better.

Interestingly, while he fixated at least part of each of the *the, though, a part,* and *should of* errors in the text, he used the expected forms—and spelled them—all correctly in his paragraph.

When talking about which errors he found in the text, he went back to look again to find as many errors as he could. He quickly found the *he, boot,* and two *the's,* but never found the other three. As you discovered this is not at all uncommon; most people do not find all six errors. But what is interesting is to look at some of Evan's fixations during his second reading of the paragraph. Part of his total eye movement record in that second reading is excerpted, below.

**Table 2.5** Evan's 2nd Reading, Searching for Errors

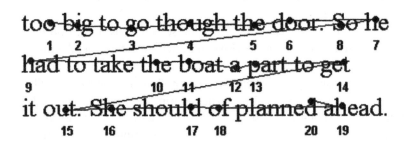

Source: reprinted from Paulson and Freeman, 2003: p.20.

In this excerpt Evan fixates *though*, *a part*, and *should of*—the three errors that he never detected. Of course, maybe he didn't identify them as errors because he doesn't know how to spell them, or use them in a sentence. But look again at his version of the paragraph that he wrote—he uses the word "through" three times, all correctly. He also spells and uses "apart" and "should have" correctly.

Let's take a closer look at what Evan did with the word "through." He spelled and used "through," correctly; in fact, he uses the word three times in his written retelling of *The Boat in the Basement*. While reading the Boat paragraph the first time, he fixated *though*, and then while reading the paragraph the second time, while searching for errors, he fixated *though* again—but never identified the word as an error. Evan's expectation of the word "through" was so strong and his construction of the text so powerful, that even while looking for anomalies he still constructed "through" instead of what was actually printed in the text.

## The Eye and the Brain

So Evan looked directly at three errors in the text, used them correctly in his written retelling, but still never found them as errors while reading. Evan is a great example of a reader so focused on meaning that even while he's looking for errors he *sees/perceives* it as if it were the correct spelling. Here again is a demonstration of the crucial difference between reading as direct input from printed page to the brain and reading as a socially constructed act focused on meaning-making.

It also shows the difference between vision and perception. If his eyes fixated on the errors in the text, the brain got that visual input. But he perceived what the brain made of that input. The brain constructed a meaningful text and in the process supplied the missing input and corrected the errors on the basis of what it expects in the language.

Like you, Evan was effective in making sense of this story. And he was efficient in selectively using the visual information to construct the meaning (make sense).

So now we can say that when you read *The Boat in the Basement* (Gollasch, 1980) you showed similar efficiency in not noticing the errors and making sense of the story. Reading is not "seeing every letter in every word." Reading is a much more efficient and complex process of making sense: constructing meaning.

## Language Patterns and Eye Movements

How does our view of language help us understand data from readers such as Evan's eye fixations shown earlier in Table 2.4?

### *Context and Predictability*

I want to emphasize two of Paulson's points (2002). He stressed the importance of context and predictability in reading. He said:

1. Context is an essential part of the reading process.

2. The more predictable a word is, the more likely it is to be skipped.

With modern computer technology it is possible to have many millions of words collected from some groups of texts such as newspapers over a period of time, transcripts of congressional hearings, etc. Each collection constitutes a *corpus*, a body of language that can be placed in a file in a laptop computer and searched using computer programs. Corpus linguistics describes patterning in language based on careful examination of corpora.

### REDUNDANCY

It is possible for readers to use context and predictability as they read because of one important aspect of language: **language is massively redundant**. That means there are strong restrictions on what can combine with what. What you say in one part of a phrase, sentence, or text, restricts the sorts of things that you can say in other parts of that same phrase, sentence, or text. Grammatical patterns illustrate one sort of restriction. In English the Subject + Verb + Object is an example. This pattern restricts what can occur in each of these functions. A word like *Henry* or *he* or *the boy* may function as subject or object but not as a verb.

| Subject | Verb | Object |
|---|---|---|
| The young boy | would have preferred | a watch. |

Words often pattern strongly with other words. For example, in a corpus of six million words, *destruction* occurs 134 times. Of that, 25 (18.7 percent) were in the phrase *weapons of mass destruction* and an additional one in the phrase *capacity for mass destruction*. The phrase *destruction of* accounts for 32 (23.9 percent) additional examples. In other words, these three sequences account for over 42 percent of the occurrences of the word *destruction* in this corpus.

Each pattern found influences the likelihood that a word of a particular type will occur. Every time such an influence on what may occur is found, we have an example of redundancy. When Evan found a pattern: *go* —— *the door* he could predict a preposition such as *through*.

## PREDICTABILITY

Since predictability is very important in our understanding of reading I want to stop and make several important points.

- Predictability **depends** on the presence of redundancy. People use the redundancy that they perceive in a text to predict, i.e., to reduce the range of options they consider likely to occur at some point in the text. The predictions they produce are based on their prior experience with the meaning the text is conveying and their knowledge of the syntactic (sentence) patterns in the language.
- When the four of us use the term *prediction*, we do **not** mean the ability to predict exactly what words will follow in the text. Rather we use *prediction* to mean the reduction of the number of options available at any particular point. For example, readers regularly preserve the grammatical class of the word they miscue on; they substitute nouns for nouns, prepositions for prepositions, adjectives for adjectives, etc. They preserve those grammatical patterns even while they are creating miscues. This ability depends on prediction.
- These predictions need not be conscious. Rather they are more typically unarticulated expectations. Every time some element is perceived, that very act of perception involves prediction in this sense. Thus perception and prediction are intimately intertwined.
- The strength of predictions ranges from expectations concerning phenomena that are:
  (a) considered highly probable (including, sometimes, predictions of exactly what follows).
  (b) among several that are quite possible.
  (c) uncommon but not surprising.

(d)  those that would be surprising if they were to occur.

(e)  impossible in this context.

We've discussed a number of places where Evan predicted what he was going to see as he fixated *The Boat in the Basement* (Gollasch, 1980). Let me continue that discussion.

## *Patterns of Language in* The Boat in the Basement

### CONTENT WORDS AND FUNCTION WORDS

English words fall into two groups. One group of words expresses most of the meaning of the sentence. Examples from the story are the nouns such as *boat* and *basement*, the main verbs such as *discovered*, *get* and *planned*, adjectives such as *big*, and some adverbs such as *apart* and *ahead*. The words in this group are all content words.

In general, content words belong to open classes. New members of open classes can be invented at any time. New nouns and verbs are regularly invented to refer to new objects and actions that we need to describe. Since the advent of computers, *boot* has become a new verb. Scientists regularly invent terms such as *quark* or *emic* to refer to objects and concepts that are relevant to their theories.

In contrast to the content words the second group of words—the function words—belong to closed classes (new ones are very unlikely) that signal grammatical relations and frame the content words. Both features make function words more predictable than content words.

Examples from the story include the articles *the* and *a*, the prepositions *in* and *through*, the helping verbs *had* and *have* (spelled <of> one time in the story), the pronouns *her, she, he* and *it*, as well as the conjunctions *when* and *so*. If we take a phrase such as *through the door* only a few words could replace *through* (*in, out, by*) or replace *the* (*a, this, that, my, his*).

But the meanings and the grammatical classes of the content words also provide some redundancy and restrict the relations that they may appear in. I'll illustrate using *The Boat in the Basement* (Gollasch, 1980) with all the function words removed.

boat basement
woman building boat

basement. finished
boat, discovered
big go door.
take boat apart get.
planned ahead

Though this text is not normal English, we can still use it as a means to construct meaning. Readers of the first sentence of the text *woman building boat basement* are likely to interpret it as implying that *woman* is the builder and *basement* is telling where the building occurred. Since the title (*boat basement*) may be interpreted as 'boat in a basement' (among other interpretations) the combination of the two (the title and the first sentence) would be likely to be taken as confirmation of this interpretation. Of course, the interpretation of the revised text will not be as complete as the original. Readers will not be secure in their interpretations because they will probably be aware of alternative interpretations at every step, just as readers and listeners are when they encounter language produced by non-native speakers of English.

Any interpretation of this text requires that readers assign a sentence pattern to know which content words are nouns, verbs, and so on. The function words make the other words predictable and thus there is redundancy: we have some information about what can and can't follow.

Evan's eye movements as he read the story show us how he treated these two types of words. *The Boat in the Basement* (Gollasch, 1980) story contains a total of 49 words. Of these, 19 are content words and 30 are function words.

The data supports the claims that Paulson made. Sixty-eight percent of the content words are fixated, while 57 percent of the function words are fixated. The content words are less predictable than the function words and are fixated at a greater rate than the function words.

## GRAMMATICAL PATTERNS

Words such as *the* and *a* occur at or near the beginning of noun phrases. When readers encounter either of these words they can predict that they will find a

**Table 2.6** Evan's Fixation Rates on Content Words and on Function Words

|  | Total words | Fixated words | Not fixated |
|---|---|---|---|
| Content words | 19 | 13 (68%) | 6 (32%) |
| Function words | 30 | 17 (57%) | 13 (43%) |
| Grand totals | 49 | 30 (61%) | 19 (39%) |

noun very soon. Further, they can predict that they won't find another instance of *the* or *a* before they find a noun. Given the strength of this restriction, it is not surprising that Evan perceived only one *the* when he first read the story.

The same sort of process occurred when Evan perceived *through* instead of *though*. *Through* and *though* are both function words, but they function in quite different ways. *Through* is a preposition and introduces noun phrases such as *through the water, through hard work*, etc. By contrast, *though* is a conjunction and introduces clauses such as *though he liked it in principle*. The closeness in spelling of *though* and *through* together with the difference in their grammatical function made *through* predictable in the pattern . . . *too big to go though the door*. Evan predicted the meaning and the grammatical pattern of a prepositional phrase and saw enough to confirm his prediction. Though he fixated on *though*, the miscue went unnoticed, even in the second reading.

## Textual Patterns

Patterns of grammar and meanings created in the text also influenced Evan's fixations on the word *boat/boot* and illustrate this sort of pattern. This text refers to the boat six times: four times using the words *boat/boot* and twice using the word *it*. Evan fixates only three of these six words: the first two occurrences of *boat* (in lines one and two), and one occurrence of *it* (in line seven).

Evan has built a meaning context: reading the first line—the title—tells him that a major topic of the story is a boat, and therefore *boat* is likely to be found frequently in the following story. We can say that the concept is predictable in the sense that readers are not surprised when the *boat* is mentioned. One consequence of that predictability is that Evan is able to perceive the word *boat* using minimal information—if you look back at Table 2.4 for the three unfixated instances of *boat/boot* and *it*, you will find that he did fixate on the words just before those unfixated instances; the blurry input from the parafovea was all he needed.

## How Does Knowledge of Language Help Us to Understand Reading?

At this point, let's return to our beginning question. How does knowledge of language help us to understand reading? How can a reader make sense of a text while not fixating on a third or more of the words?

The common view of language is that texts consist primarily of words, and that the receptive processing of texts—reading and listening—consists primarily of sequentially identifying and interpreting the words in the text and seeing how they are related. But the view that words are like bricks laid one on one to construct our messages is wrong. Rather words participate in language patterns of various sizes and natures. The words themselves take different shapes and textures depending on the contexts in which they are found.

In dealing with *The Boat in the Basement* (Gollasch, 1980) both you and Evan made sense of the text and failed to see the embedded errors because your focus was on making sense. Perceiving the language patterns (for example imposing an appropriate grammatical structure on a sentence) is critical to understanding the text. But there is no need to specifically identify each and every word in a pattern to perceive the pattern, any more than it is necessary to identify all the letters in a word in order to perceive the word. Patterns may be perceived based on partial information and then used to fill in the missing information. That's the source of our grand illusion.

We need to make a very important point to sum up this discussion. We'll say it in this book many times: reading is a process of making sense of written language. So when we talk about context we are talking about the way all the information available to the reader is used to make sense—to get to the meaning. Paulson made a key point: if we needed to fixate on every word, we would.

Peter has shown us that much of language consists of patterns of words—formulaic language—that are highly predictable. Once you are aware of the pattern, the grammar and the phrasing make it possible to be very efficient in getting to meaning.

Effective reading is making sense of what we are reading. Efficient reading is getting the meaning with the least amount of visual input. The speed of reading is not in itself important. Efficiency is what produces the speed and that involves using minimal information from the text. So we only fixate enough to get the meaning. And once we get meaning, the grand illusion follows. We think we have seen all the words and, indeed, in oral reading we are able to produce a coherent text which will come close to the printed text.

# References

Dodge, R. (1900). "Visual perceptions during eye movement." *Psychological Review*, VII, 454–465.

Duckett, P. (2008). "Seeing the story for the words: The eye-movements of beginning readers." In Flurkey, A., Paulson, E., and Goodman, K. (Eds.), *Scientific realism in studies of reading.* (pp. 113–128). New York: Lawrence Erlbaum Associates.

Fisher, D. and Shebilske, W. (1985). "There is more that meets the eye than the eye assumption." In Groner, R., McConkie, G., and Menz, C. (Eds.), *Eye movements and human information processing* (pp. 149–157). Amsterdam: Elsevier Science Publishers B.V.

Gollasch, F. (1980). *Readers' perceptions in detecting and processing embedded errors in meaningful text.* (Doctoral dissertation). Retrieved from ProQuest Dissertations and Theses database (UMI No. 8107445).

Hogaboam, T. W. (1983). "Reading patterns in eye movement data." In Rayner, K. (Ed.), *Eye movements in reading: Perceptual and language processes* (pp. 309–332). New York: Academic.

Javal, E. (1882). *Notice sur les travaux scientifiques de Émile Javal.* Paris: Gauthier-Villars et fils.

Judd, C. H. and Buswell, G. T. (1922). *Silent reading: a study of the various types.* Chicago: University of Chicago.

Just, M. and Carpenter, P. (1987). *The psychology of reading and language comprehension.* Newton, MA: Allyn & Bacon.

Kim, K., Knox, M., and Brown, J. (2007). "Eye movement and strategic reading." In Goodman, Y. M. and Martens, P. (Eds.), *Critical issues in early literacy: Research and pedagogy* (pp. 47–57). Mahwah, NJ: Lawrence Erlbaum Associates.

Paulson, E. J. (2002). "Are oral reading word omissions and substitutions caused by careless eye movements?" *Reading Psychology, 23*(1), 45–66.

Paulson, E. J., Flurkey, A. D., Goodman, Y. M. and Goodman, K. S. (2003). "Eye movements and miscue analysis: Reading from a constructivist perspective." In Fairbanks, C., Worthy, J., Maloch, B., Hoffman, J., and Schallert, D. (Eds.), *The yearbook of the national reading conference, 52,* 345–355. Oak Creek, WI: National Reading Conference.

Paulson, E. J. and Freeman, A. E. (2003). *Insight from the eyes: The science of effective reading instruction.* Portsmouth, NH: Heinemann.

Rayner, K. (1997). "Understanding eye movements in reading," *Scientific Studies of Reading, 1*(4), 317–339.

Rayner, K. and Pollatsek, A. (1989). *The psychology of reading.* Englewood Cliffs, NJ: Prentice Hall.

Wolverton, G. S. and Zola, D. (1983). "The temporal characteristics of visual information extraction during reading." In Rayner, K. (Ed.), *Eye movements in reading: Perceptual and language processes* (pp. 41–51). New York: Academic.

# Reading with Our Brains   **3**

Think about these seemingly simple things we humans do all the time.

When I take a step in the dark, I can't wait until I have moved to know what my step will result in. I predict on the best hunch I have—call it prior knowledge, or intuition, or a good guess. And all of us have been surprised when we expected a step that wasn't there or encountered a step we hadn't expected.

When a right fielder in baseball leaps for a fly ball on the dead run and catches it, he could not leap toward where the ball is. It's moving rapidly. He predicts where it will be and his brain sends instructions to his muscles where to take him to intercept the trajectory of the ball.

And when I read, I can't recognize words and then decide what they mean. I have to predict a grammatical pattern and wording, decide on the basis of what I know what is likely to follow, and do it so efficiently that my sense is that I am reading not words but the meaning I construct as I make sense of the written language.

All of these occurrences show a brain that is predicting on the basis of what it already knows. When, many years ago I said that reading was a "psycholinguistic guessing game" (Goodman, 1967), what I had discovered is that as we read, our brains are always a step ahead. The predictions our brains make as we read are educated guesses and we either confirm them and proceed, or we disconfirm them and regress to get more information. Prediction is essential to everything we do.

## Consistency of Our View of Reading with Developing Brain Theory

Ken's transactional, sociopsycholinguistic model of reading is based on extensive study of what readers do with real texts (Goodman and Goodman, 2014). This already distinguishes his model from many others, whose research concerns are letters, words, or nonsense syllables presented in isolation and out of context, and whose theoretical premise is that accurate perception of letters and words is a prerequisite to proficient reading.

In this section I'll show that Ken's model of reading is fully consistent with what we know about the psychology of illusions and the fundamental distinction that needs to be drawn between the contents of consciousness and the subconscious mechanisms that manufacture those contents (see Chapter 4).

We observed that a full explanation of illusions, including the illusions of reading, combine together concepts from both psychology and neuroscience; we can now also say that *the transactional, sociopsycholinguistic model of reading* is consistent with the known biology of the human brain. For this reason, we could call Ken's model of reading a *sociopsycho-neurolinguistic* model: it is consistent with neurological theory as well.

### The Virtual and the Real

Our assertion that the virtual reality our brains construct (what we think we see) is more important than what the eyes

 Miscue analysis research produced a developing model of the reading process: what happens when people read. As the model developed, I called it linguistic. Soon it became obvious that it was psycholinguistic, meaning that both language and thought were involved. Our work with different dialect groups made it a sociopsycholinguistic model. Now Steve is saying "but it also involves neurology." Thus it is a transactional neurosocio-psycholinguistic model or a socioneuropsycholinguistic model or a sociopsycho-neurolinguistic model. Let's make it easy and call it a comprehensive model of the reading process.

actually see is in no way a defense of sloppy disregard for reality or empirical truth. Indeed, it is just the opposite. Reality is too complex for our sensing nervous system; it cannot fully detect that reality. But the brain provides a biological advantage; it constructs a coherent reality from the imperfect input. People must make split-second decisions based on less than complete information.

To the sensing mind, accuracy is hardly a simple, straightforward, or immediately available relationship with the objective world. Accuracy in perception is, in any case, always tentative because it is based on a prediction, and may be disconfirmed by new evidence. The coarse and crude character of the sense organs falls far short of what can actually be perceived. The rest must be filled in by the brain itself. The brain predicts what it will see and hear. These predictions are guesses, and the better the guess, the closer we are to accurate perception. When accuracy does indeed characterize the perception, it is not because of what the eyes see, it is because our brains have predicting mechanisms that make really good guesses.

Still, the relationship between making sense and empirical accuracy is far from arbitrary, because making sense means bringing order and pattern to what we perceive. Our sensory detectors sample from the real world. As we have seen, however, it is impossible for the brain to make sense of that reality without inserting some of its own nature into the contents of consciousness. The brain uses its background knowledge, its beliefs, and its motives to make sense of the imperfect input. The final product is the individual's unique (but socially constrained) mental representation of the world.

## Making Sense Is the Preferred State of the Human Brain

Because our nervous system possesses the capacity to create coherent meaning, making sense functions as a stamp of approval. When we have made sense of what we are seeing, hearing, and feeling, we believe that our perception of reality is true, whether it is or isn't. I really did see a yellow sign or I really did see the player get tagged out at home. The feeling that goes along with a sense of having made sense of the world is usually taken for granted. But everyone knows the feeling of being confused, of believing that the world is not being accurately perceived, of seeing mutually incoherent objects or hearing mutually incoherent sounds, or of seeing things and hearing sounds that don't match our knowledge and beliefs about the world. This feeling of confusion is not a pleasant one. The feeling of making sense is. But the former is precisely the nail we step on that informs us that *making sense is the preferred state of the human brain*, just as unimpeded breathing is the preferred state of the lungs.

The feeling that accompanies the belief that we have been accurate in our perceptions does not depend on actually having been accurate. What we are capable of believing is not constrained by empirical accuracy or scientifically verified sense.

## Making Sense Is Itself an Illusion

We believe we have made sense if there is a feeling that informs us of that. The sense we have made *works*—it is useful. Human cultures are filled with irrational beliefs that feel quite believable, hence quite sensible and accurate. There is a sense of conviction that goes along with such beliefs, no matter how demonstrably false they may be. Battles are fought between opposing "truths."

### Qualia

Neuroscientists talk about "qualia." These are the feelings that accompany certain sensory experiences, the feeling that accompanies seeing something yellow as opposed to green, or hearing something musical as opposed to something cacaphonous. We don't just perceive yellow; we feel yellowness.

The notion of qualia can be extended to the phenomenon of making sense. We do not merely perceive colored objects, nor do we merely arrange them in visual space. We make sense of that arrangement—a bowl of cherries, a burning candle, spilled milk, ink blotches. But even more, we have a feeling that accompanies that sense-making, that signals that coherent sense has been achieved, and, again, we know this indirectly by the alternate feeling that accompanies confusion.

Making sense can be driven by a variety of things that may conflict with "objective" reality: the hope that something is true; the rewarding feeling of community and social bonding that accompanies shared belief; the feeling of sanity that accompanies shared belief; the distortions based on pathologic, delusional thinking. A schizophrenic believes that a martian is in his brain just as surely as you believe there isn't. This doesn't make both beliefs equally true. There is no martian in anyone's brain. But the conviction is equally strong.

So there is a difference that needs to be appreciated between empirical accuracy and making sense, and between making sense and the qualia we call conviction. Each difference is responsible for its own type of illusion. The difference between empirical accuracy and making sense creates the illusion of empirical accuracy. The difference between making sense and conviction creates the illusion of having made sense.

The dynamic relationships among perception, sense-making, and belief constitute the fundamental mode of human thought. These relationships pose quintessential questions: why is making conceptual sense necessary in order to achieve a sense of accurate perception? Why is conviction necessary in order to achieve a sense of having made sense?

The answer to these questions exposes the balancing act performed by the human mind. There is no independent, separate mental observer in the brain verifying the accuracy of our perceptions and then informing us as to whether or not our perceptions were accurate. There is no independent, separate mental observer in the brain checking that we have truly made sense, that all the *i*'s are dotted and *t*'s are crossed. The voice that tells us we are accurate in our perceptions belongs to the same self that is doing the perceiving and believing in the sense it has constructed. This voice says "I believe that I have made sense, therefore I have accurately perceived."

## A New Paradigm: The Neuroscience of Constructive Psychology

All of this psychology and philosophy is beginning to be supported by scientific studies of the brain's internal workings. No doubt we are quite far from a satisfying neuroscientific account of the dynamic interactions among belief, sense-making, and perception. But the outlines of a paradigm are emerging: a paradigm that expresses the neuroscience of constructivist psychology.

Such a paradigm was already anticipated years ago by Ken Goodman. With Yetta Goodman (1978), he wrote:

> The brain is always anticipating and predicting as it seeks order and significance in sensory inputs. . . . If the brain predicts, it must also seek to verify its predictions. So it monitors to confirm or disconfirm with subsequent input what it expected. . . . The brain reprocesses when it finds inconsistencies or its predictions are disconfirmed. . . . These processes have an intrinsic sequence. Prediction precedes confirmation which precedes correction. Yet the same information may be used to confirm a prior prediction and make a new one.
>
> (1978, pp. 2–6)

At the time, there was hardly an understanding of how the brain could accomplish these feats. But does that mean that the Goodmans were not entitled to make such a statement? Of course they were, because they had discovered that reading involves making sense of print, that the mechanism of making sense involves predicting and confirming or disconfirming those predictions via a transaction with the text, and that accepting the sense so constructed involves accommodating it to a belief system. In other words, they were making an empirical prediction, on the basis of their reading miscue research with a wide range of ages, that the brain contains circuits that allow it to formulate and test conceptual and propositional predictions.

## Evidence from Invertebrates

Their predictions are now bearing fruit. Neuroscientists are beginning to work out the neural circuits and mechanisms involved in constructing sense. And surprisingly some of the evidence is coming from studies of lower species—even invertebrates.

Let's consider crickets. Male crickets generate sound bursts by closing their wings rhythmically. There is a neural pathway that runs from the contractile apparatus of the wings to the cricket's auditory apparatus. With each closing of the wings, a signal is sent to this auditory center. The nervous signal inhibits the auditory response of the male cricket to its own wing closings. Entomologists believe that this mechanism prevents ordinary desensitization from occurring, such as occurs in humans when we no longer detect a foul smell that surrounds us. In this way, the male cricket remains ready to hear the sounds of other males in the area.

The cricket has a built-in neural mechanism that allows its auditory apparatus to anticipate that when the sound of wing closure is heard, it will be that of another male cricket. There is a functional utility in this mechanism. If it did not exist, the cricket would lose its ability to hear others of its species because its own sound-producing mechanism would trigger desensitization. Biologist Barbara Webb (2004) calls this biological phenomenon a "predictive transformation." Similarly, Webb shows that a cockroach that needs to escape rapidly must know the current positions of its limbs in order to best decide which way to turn and scurry away. It has proprioceptive sensors that inform its nervous system of exactly these positions. But computing position based on proprioceptive feedback "may be too slow to serve this function." Researchers have proposed that the cockroach, in performing a movement, simultaneously predicts the proprioceptive consequence of that movement, and that it uses this prediction to make its next move, rather than go through the proprioceptive calculations from scratch.

In this way the cockroaches are "able to predict the sensory consequences of their actions to be capable of rapid, robust, and adaptive behavior." This ability of roaches demonstrates that the phenomenon of prediction applies not only to intellectual life but to raw motor life as well.

## Forward Model

This concept is called a *forward model*. In forward models, there "is an internal loop that takes the motor command, and predicts the expected sensory input which can be used to modulate the processing of the actual input."

### INTERNAL LOOP

There are two crucial features to this model. The first is the notion of an "internal loop," in which neural information moves back and forth between the center and the periphery, that is to say, between the organism and its environment. The center issues a motor command to move in a certain direction at a certain speed. The periphery collects data on the position of the organism's joints in space. These data keep the center informed and guide the organism's particular motor settings.

### PREDICTIVE TRANSFORMATION

The second feature is the "predictive transformation." The motor command from the center not only connects to all the relevant muscle cells but to the very proprioceptive sensors that relay joint position information. On the basis of the motor command, proprioceptive dials are set *in advance of actual proprioceptive information arriving from the periphery*. This setting of the dials constitutes a prediction on what physical posture the organism will be in once it has carried out its motor command.

But the prediction may or may not be true. An unanticipated dip in the ground can alter that posture from the outside. In that case, the predicted proprioceptive settings will not be the same as the actual proprioceptive settings—the anticipated posture of the organism is not its actual posture. The expected setting is compared to the observed setting, and the organism can now "modulate the processing of the actual input."

Similarly, flying insects compare the predicted position of their wings to the actual position which may be altered by unexpected gusts of wind. The observed position either confirms or disconfirms the expected position. In the former case, the motor commands continue as previously set up. In the latter case, they are modulated. The desired trajectory stays on target.

You might question the efficiency of such a system, whether it can achieve Webb's "rapid" and "robust" decision-making calculations. It seems that the organism still has to go through the proprioceptive calculations that were claimed to be relatively inefficient when carried out repeatedly before each new movement. But the availability of a proprioceptive quotient already *predicted* by the inner loop allows a minimum number of *actual* proprioceptive quantities to be assessed by the organism. Only a small number needs to be sampled and compared to the predicted values in order for the organism to decide on its next move. A match means "proceed as previously planned." A mismatch means "change course."

In the inner loop "predictive transformation" model, there is a constant back-and-forth, give-and-take exchange of neural information. Center-to-periphery and periphery-to-center constitute integrated circuits.

The neuroscientific explanation of how a motor command works cannot be understood in isolation and out of context from the sensory information which keeps it on track. And it is precisely the capacity to make adjustments, by comparing expected postures to observed postures, for example, that demonstrates the *purposeful* nature of the act. The capacity to revise one's motor command to accommodate new information reveals that even the cockroach is far more than an automaton.

How much greater and more dynamic must be the non-automatic, purposeful, willful acts of linguistic beings like us, of beings who are conscious of being conscious.

## But What Does Locomotion of a Bug Have in Common with Thinking and Reading?

What we mean by action can include not just physical movement but the movement of thought as well, that is to say, the construction of mental representations. A forward model explanation for both the motor behavior of "lower cognitive" organisms and the mental behavior of "higher cognitive" organisms strongly suggests that it is a biologically fundamental characteristic of nervous systems in invertebrates, vertebrates, and beings with language and thought. In other words, it is a template that has retained its overall architecture throughout evolution. It not only permits movement to be "rapid, robust, and adaptive," but thought as well.

Our fielder going for the ball starts in to meet the batted ball. He has misjudged the speed it is coming at him yet he is ready to correct, adapting to catch it while moving away from the oncoming ball.

What does it mean to say that thought is "rapid, robust, and adaptive?" There must be a strong component of efficiency and non-randomness. A full explanation must show how the motor pathways of the nervous system work. It must also show how the peripheral detectors keep the motor commands or thoughts on a trajectory toward their goal. Without a full loop, center-to-periphery and periphery-to-center, thought would be inefficient and random. Only chance would lead the organism to its target.

Reading also involves continuous revaluing of information from the printed text to confirm or disconfirm predictions, adjust for unexpected input, correct or regress and keep the focus on meaning. The more efficiently we do this—with the least amount of time and effort—the more effective we will be in building meaning.

## What Does It Mean for the Brain to be Focused?

What keeps thought efficiently on track? The facts of the matter have been there all along, waiting to be properly interpreted. To consider these facts, we need to have some terminology to talk about the brain and how it works.

In the human brain all sensory information other than smell is picked up by special receptors and then sent to an organ deep in the brain called the *thalamus*. The eyes send visual information to one part of the thalamus. The ears send auditory information to another part. The skin sends tactile information to still another area in the thalamus. (The olfactory sense—our very primitive sense of smell—bypasses the thalamus and goes directly to the limbic system.)

### The Role of the Thalamus

The thalamus in turn sends sensory information to particular areas of the cortex, the outer cell layers of the brain that are crucial for higher cognitive function.

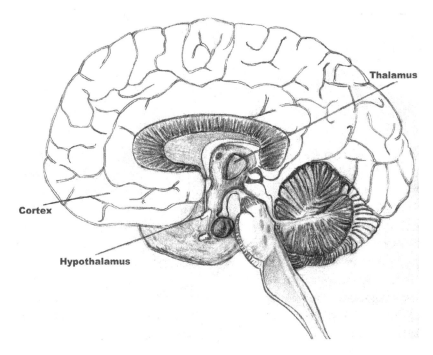

**Figure 3.1** The Thalamus. Original art by Shoshana Pearson

Visual information goes to the occipital lobes in the back of the brain. Auditory information goes to the temporal lobes on either side of the brain. Tactile information goes to the parietal lobes over the upper outer regions of the brain. From these areas of the cortex, the sensory information is used to generate perceptions. The sensory input is transformed by the cortex into perceptions: what we see, hear, and feel become what we think we see, hear, and feel. In the introduction Ken talked about different uses of *see*. What the mind perceives is based on more than what the eyes *see*: it is what the brain makes of it.

In traditional neuroscience teaching, the thalamus has been described as the "gatekeeper" or "relay station" for sensory information coming into the brain from outside. Sensory information is collected by the sense organs, sent to the cortex by the thalamus, and then processed by increasingly abstract cortical regions to form percepts, concepts, propositions, and experiences.

But that would mean human experience, the human essence, is a fundamentally passive one in the world. Such models process information. In these models, accurate letter and word identification precedes meaning construction.

Lines and curves are processed by a letter-identifying program. Letters are turned into sounds by a phonological processing program. Sounds are melded together by a word-identification program. Words are melded together by a syntactic program. Eventually you get to meaning as you travel across the cortex. But that can't be what happens. The time for all that to happen would itself make it impossible.

## Feedback and Feed-Forward

A significant feature of how our brains are constructed raises an important challenge to this view, for not only are there nerve tracts running from the thalamus to the cortex, sending sensory information to higher levels, but there are also nerve tracts running from the cortex to the thalamus. Traditionally, these pathways have been referred to as *feedback* pathways. Their function in the overall system has been thought of as a kind of braking mechanism on the bottom-up flow of information. Conversely, the neural pathways that send information from the thalamus to the cortex have been called *feed-forward* pathways. The very terms *feedback* and *feed-forward* betray a definite scientific point of view—that the outside-in or bottom-up pathways are primary, and the inside-out or top-down pathways are secondary.

Along with leading neuroscientists, we reject this view. We don't question the existence of thalamocortical and corticothalamic pathways (from cortex to thalamus and from thalamus to cortex). These are established neuro-anatomical facts. What we reject is the one direction of interpretation of the functions of the pathways. Here is a curious fact that is one reason why we reject the traditional interpretation: there are actually ten times as many corticothalamic fibers sending signals *from the cortex to the thalamus* as there are thalamocortical fibers sending signals from the thalamus to the cortex. This is distinctly odd and entirely unexpected if the primary pathway were indeed periphery-to-center (thalamocortical).

Neuroscientists have recently formulated the problem this way: if the cortex to thalamus pathway plays the dominant, primary role in human psychology, that is, in connecting abstract conceptualization regions of the brain to sensory information, then this pathway is *the neural mechanism for predicting*. In this role, it is the feed-forward part of the brain. The brain is not waiting for visual input; it is formulating hypotheses about the world and then telling the eyes where to look and what to look for. And that, of course, is what Ken's reading model is all about.

## The Organ of Prediction and Confirmation

We are talking about a revolutionary change currently taking place in the field of neuroscience. Another leading neuroanatomist has concluded that "the descending corticothalamic information could therefore be a 'prediction' of the sensory input." (Destexhe, 2000: 405). Just as in reading, predictions control the process of making sense of the world.

Summarizing these new understandings, Hawkins and Blakeslee conclude that "The cortex is an organ of prediction" (2004: 89). It follows that the thalamocortical pathways constitute the organ of confirmation and disconfirmation. Hawkins and Blakeslee (2004) also observe that purposeful movements inherently involve making predictions and confirming or disconfirming them. Reaching for a doorknob involves anticipating the feel and shape of the knob, proceeding with one's movements when no surprises are encountered such as expecting the door to be unlocked and finding that the knob turns smoothly, and correcting and revising one's motor plan when something unanticipated is encountered—the door being locked, for example.

Sherman, Guillery, and Sherman (2006) also observe that the new insights regarding the thalamus and cerebral cortex may help solve the problem of the "close link between action and perception," a problem that has "long puzzled philosophers, psychologists, and psychophysicists" (p. 25–26). The key is precisely what Hawkins and Blakeslee (2004) suggest, that purposeful movements are motor patterns guided by, and corrected by, predictions and that these predictions arise in the cortex, specifically, in the frontal lobe, where motor planning is thought to occur, and navigated by the thalamocortical fibers functioning as a system subordinate to the corticothalamic connections.

## Evidence for Kinesiology

Not all scientists, though, have been puzzled by the problem of action and perception. Purposeful movements have been the subject matter of empirical study in the branch of neuroscience called kinesiology. Kinesiologists consider phenomena like reaching for an object with your hand. Suppose you are reaching for an egg. It is very curious that, for the most part, when you know you are reaching for an egg you do not grab it so hard that the egg will crush as your hand grasps it. Or suppose you are reaching for a tiny pebble. Your hand, in advance of arriving at the object, has already assumed a smaller caliber than what it would assume were it reaching for an egg. Kinesiologists divide the purposeful movement of the upper extremity into three components—

transport, grasp, and manipulation. The transport component drives the large muscles of the arm and forearm and sends the extremity, and the hand attached to it, toward the goal. The grasp component creates the posture of the hand appropriate to the size and shape of the object. The manipulation component adapts the motor forces of the fingers to the surface characteristics of the object. So the right fielder catching the ball on the run closes his glove on the ball with just enough force to keep it from falling out.

For an object of a given size, the duration of the transport phase is quite stable. The velocity of the movement varies depending on distance of the object from the starting point of the hand, but the time to reach peak velocity is stable at about 60–70 percent of that distance. The time to maximum opening of the hand for grasping is invariant over variable distances. Interestingly, the transport phase of the movement becomes longer as the size of the object becomes smaller. The increased time to grasping is found in the slower deceleration phase of the transport movement, and is thought to be related to the precision required in reaching the target.

Kinesiologists have interpreted these robust findings as evidence for the existence of a brain-based program for reaching and grasping. The program controls the speed and direction of the extremity as it transports the hand, as well as the speed of opening and aperture size of the grip. All of this occurs with empirically documented on-line utilization of sensory information. A widely held theory is that the overall movement is guided by a mental representation of the object to be grasped. This representation contains information about the object's extrinsic and intrinsic properties. Extrinsic properties have to do with its location in space, that is, its distance from the hand. Intrinsic properties have to do with its shape, size, color, and so on. Once grasped, the manipulation phase which regulates the force of hand muscles applied to the object is guided by sensory information about its texture, firmness, temperature, and so on.

The guidance system at work in human upper extremity trajectories, in which the transport system is regulated by extrinsic visual information, the grasp system by intrinsic visual information, and the manipulation system by non-visual sensory information, has been well worked out on the basis of studies using experiments of nature, for example, individuals with a variety of neurologic disorders that impair one or more of the sensory systems, and of studies on primates with similar trajectory behaviors. Kinesiologists have noted that not only do the sensory systems guide the motor trajectory, but they also constitute an "error-correcting mechanism" for trajectories that fail. The important thing to notice here is that the outside-in, bottom-up visual pathways which project information about the location of the object along a "dorsal stream" to the parietal lobe, and the nature of the object along a "ventral stream" to the temporal lobe, is not a feed-forward system, but rather a feedback system. The movements themselves are the result of a feed-forward system.

Therefore, the phenomenon of purposeful movement is a well-established area of neuroscience in which *bottom-up neurons constitute the feedback system*. The fibers that begin in the cortical surface, in this case in the frontal lobe where motor plans are formulated, constitute the feed-forward system. By feed-forward we mean they anticipate and precede the input rather than responding to the input.

## It's the Cortex that Makes Sense!

All this puts us in a position to understand why there are ten times as many corticothalamic fibers as thalamocortical fibers. **Processing sensory information is subordinate to an even higher function of the brain—making sense of the world.** The brain, as Ken said long ago, is engaged in a guessing game (Goodman, 1967). It accomplishes this, in part, by formulating guesses about aspects of the perceivable world. It tests its guesses by granting access to selected sensory features of the world. The part of the brain that formulates the guesses is the cortex, the evolutionarily most advanced organ on the planet. The part of the brain that transmits sensory information to the cortex is the thalamus. The cortex communicates with the thalamus via corticothalamic fibers. The thalamus communicates with the cortex via thalamocortical fibers. The former far outnumber the latter because the cortex is in charge of the highest levels of brain function.

Here's an example. The cortex decides to look for its car in the parking lot. Instead of waiting for the thalamus to detect red—the color of the car it is looking for—it directs the thalamus to search for red. It may do this, for example, by inhibiting cells that detect other colors. In any case, not every single physical characteristic of the car needs to be detected before the cortex can conclude that it has found the car it is looking for. A condition requiring such a degree of accuracy would never allow a mental task to terminate. But in detecting red, the thalamus has found the evidence it needs to keep the cortex's mental activity on track. Is it possible that the cortex mistakenly concludes that the red car in the corner of the parking lot is the one it is looking for? Of course. The disconfirmatory evidence may be the out-of-state license plate. The cortex has to revise its tentative conclusion that it found the car. It will then direct the thalamus to obtain additional information.

It is all just a series of guesses, however well-guided they may be by memory, background knowledge, and background beliefs (I remember that I parked my car on 42nd street, I know that it is red, and I believe that it has not transmogrified into a horse). And this reveals another illusion, one that applies as much to reading as it does to every other instantiation of brain activity in the world.

Focusing on the subordinate functions of the brain, advocates of phonological processing see proficiency as the phenomenon whereby learned behaviors become highly automatic. Focusing on the highest levels of the brain, advocates of a transactional model of reading see proficiency as the phenomenon whereby the guessing becomes so good that it creates the illusion of not having made a really good guess, but of just being right.

## Billions of Loops

These successful guesses are not automatic, even though they are made with amazing speed taking into account all complex factors that influence our transactions with the world around us. Understanding the phenomenon of guessing as being responsible for the illusion of firmly knowing is the subject matter of empirical science, and ranks as a major scientific discovery.

It remains to be seen whether inverting the traditional understanding of the relationship between corticothalamic and thalamocortical pathways, that is, between traditional feed-forward and feedback neural events, results in the same galactic scientific and psychological reverberation as was achieved when the sun and the Earth switched places in our understanding of orbits in the solar system. The obstacle to spreading the astronomical truth was not science itself, but social systems and the beliefs they demanded of people.

In any case, the real paradigm change lies in appreciating that the bi-directional pathways constitute integrated, neural loops that constitute the basis for constructing mental representations of reality. In other words, the loops—billions and billions of them, some fixed and some newly created—are the basic architecture of constructivist neuroscience, the brain basis of constructivist psychology.

In paying attention to and actually anticipating cutting-edge developments in neuroscience, it is clear that the meaning-based model of reading derives support from brain biology. Independent of studies of reading, we are now beginning to understand that the brain is hard-wired to predict and then confirm and disconfirm its predictions. The brain would have to be quite a different kind of organ for reading to not be an instantiation of this general phenomenon.

## Convergence

A paradigmatic convergence of monumental proportions is occurring between psychology and neuroscience. This convergence will tip the scales of scientific inquiry into human nature in favor of models that recognize **the active contribution of the mind to its interaction with the environment**. It is scientifically revolutionary because it proposes the material basis for understanding why humans are not merely passive responders to the outside world, but rather subjects of their own experiences. In my opinion, such models will resonate with scientists and lay people only when we have constructed a fundamentally freer society than the one we have now, a society which does not benefit from people feeling helpless in the face of authority, from feeling like objects of their own lives rather than subjects. In a truly free society, constructivist psychology and neuroscience will feel like common sense.

## Who Denies Biology?

In this book we've avoided where possible arguing against views that disagree with our own. However, there has been so much discussion in the press of claims that brain research supports teaching of phonics that we decided we should critique this research. In her bestselling, popular book *Overcoming Dyslexia: A New and Complete Science-Based Program for Reading Problems at Any Level* (2003), Sally Shaywitz criticizes whole language, meaning-centered approaches to reading. She says that "self-appointed opinion makers . . . ascribe children's reading problems entirely to sociological or educational factors and totally deny the biology" (Shaywitz, 2003: 4). Of course she means Ken.

This rejection of a meaning-making approach is not new. In 1994, Keith Stanovich wrote:

> That direct instruction in alphabetic coding facilitates early reading acquisition is one of the most well established conclusions in all of behavioral science. . . . The idea that learning to read is just like learning to speak is accepted by no responsible linguist, psychologist, or cognitive scientist in the research community.
>
> (pp. 285–286)

Shaywitz and Stanovich avoid dealing with the substantive issues by marginalizing the credibility of those whose views differ from theirs.

Mathematicians solve theorems every day. How does the brain do this? It is perfectly reasonable to assert that the brain considers the theorem's axioms and premises, employs principles of logical reasoning, and recruits mechanisms that create new insights into how logic connects the axioms to the final proposition. In reading, can comprehension be a simple response to identifying words on a page? Doesn't making sense require bringing meaning to the page in order to construct meaning from it?

Neurobiologists study the synaptic basis of learning because psychology has informed them of the phenomenon of learning. Neurobiologists study the cerebral elements of language because psychologists and linguists have informed them of the existence of language. And neurobiologists study the brain's capacity to read because those who study reading have explained to them what reading is. In truth, any criticism that certain reading researchers "ignore the biology" must really be a criticism of the theory of reading that those researchers support, not a criticism of their views of biology or their ascribed status as scholars.

So let's consider the principles of reading of those who regard reading as non-language. From their writings I've derived eight principles of the phonological processing model of reading and its biological foundation:

**Principle 1**   Reading is nothing more or less than the identification of written words. (We take that up in more depth in Chapter 5.)

> Unless the processes involved in individual word recognition operate properly, nothing else in the system can either.
>
> (Adams, 1990, p. 6).

**Principle 2**   The identification of a written word proceeds by breaking the word apart into its component letters, then sounding out the letters using well-known phonics patterns: "phonological processing."

> [T]o read a word, the reader must first segment the word into its underlying phonologic elements.
>
> (Shaywitz, 1998: pp. 307–308)

> The task of the reader is to transform the visual percepts of alphabetic script into linguistic ones—that is, to recode graphemes (letters) into their corresponding phonemes. To accomplish this, the beginning reader must first come to a conscious awareness of the internal phonological structure of spoken words. Then he or she must realize that the orthography—the sequence of letters on the page—represents this phonology. That is precisely what happens when a child learns to read.
>
> (Shaywitz, 1996: pp. 99–100)

**Principle 3** Word identification via letter-sound conversion proceeds without recourse to any contextual information.

> Scientific research, however, simply does not support the claim that context and authentic text are a proxy for decoding skills. To guess the pronunciation of words from context, the context must predict the words. But content words—the most important words for text comprehension—can be predicted from surrounding context only 10 to 20 percent of the time . . . Instead, the choice strategy for beginning readers is to decode letters to sounds in an increasingly complete and accurate manner.
>
> (Lyon, 1998: p. 17)

**Principle 4** Having turned a visual word into its spoken form, the reader can now enter the language system of the brain. The brain is hard-wired to only accept oral language because oral language is the only natural form of language. Writing systems are an artificial, late-appearing language form, a non-universal achievement of certain cultures, not a universal achievement of biological evolution.

> Although both speaking and reading rely on phonological processing, there is a significant difference: speaking is natural, and reading is not. Reading is an invention and must be learned at a conscious level.
>
> (Shaywitz, 1996: p. 98)

> The reader must somehow convert the print on a page into a linguistic code—the phonetic code, the only code recognized and accepted by the language system of the brain . . . Having been translated into the phonetic code, printed words are now accepted by the neural circuitry already in place for processing spoken language. Decoded into phonemes, words are processed automatically by the language system.
>
> (Shaywitz, 2003: pp. 50–51)

**Principle 5** There are specific sites in the brain where phonological processing occurs.

> Some people are lacking or weak in this processing and thus are dyslexic. Evidence of abnormal activation of these sites is evidence of dyslexia.
>
> (Shaywitz, 2003)

**Principle 6**   Intensive phonics instruction can repair a dyslexic brain (Shaywitz, 2003).

**Principle 7**   The biological basis of dyslexia can be seen in physical discrepancies between the brains of proficient and dyslexic readers.

**Principle 8**   The biological basis of these discrepancies lies in genetics.

> [R]ecent studies have shown that not only does dyslexia run in families but it is carried as a genetic trait.
>
> (Shaywitz et al., 1996: p. 99)

## *Response to this Paradigm*

The first three principles are strictly about reading, and are logically independent of any of the subsequent biological claims. Indeed, they historically arose long before the advent of modern neuroimaging technology, the main piece of technology used to investigate the phonological processing model of reading.

We demonstrated in Chapter 1 that readers do not even fixate on about a third of words, so they cannot possibly be identifying all the letters in all the words to read. Forty years of research on what real readers do turns claims about accuracy and letter-sound conversion into theoretical embarrassments.

As you, our readers, observed in your own reading, proficient readers do *not* identify all words. Any theory of reading must explain why, and of the ones they look at, many are in fact omitted in oral reading, or replaced with other words. We have learned that the subjective impression we may have that we read each word on the page is an illusion. We think we see what our brains expected to see on the basis of what it already knows.

The alleged conversion of written words into their spoken counterparts via rules of phonics is also an illusion. The phonics rules typically taught in classrooms work for a small fraction of the words encountered in a text. One of the most curious and theoretically embarrassing aspects of the phonics view of reading is that its most ardent supporters have never worked out the patterns that developing readers allegedly employ. In order to get them to work on all the words, they would have to be so complex that it would be more difficult to learn them than to learn how to read (Strauss, 2005; Venezky, 1993).

Word identification outside of context also contradicts the facts of reading and of language in general. As Eric Paulson has demonstrated in his eye movement studies, even if we took word identification to be an established principle of reading, the conclusion we must draw from the empirical fact that so many words are actually not even looked at is that word identification often proceeds *only* by using context. In Chapter 6, our discussion of the nature of words shows word meanings are interpreted and are crucially dependent on the phrases and the grammatical contexts in which they occur.

The remaining biological principles are no less absurd. If the brain were hard-wired to accept only oral language, then sign language would have to be first converted into a spoken form to be processed. But how could that happen if deaf people have never heard the sounds. The naturalness with which deaf children learn to sign is empirical evidence that what is hard-wired is the capacity of the brain to manipulate symbolic systems.

Indeed, the fundamental distinction between written and oral language is not its outer form, visual versus oral. Rather, it is that they have distinct temporal and spatial characteristics. What is common to both is the use of systems of abstract symbols to represent the world and our experiences with it. And human beings are uniquely equipped to create such systems. We can represent nature and our understandings of it. In doing so, we do not alter the reality of what we are experiencing—we never alter the laws of nature. And the brain has no more difficulty figuring out what an unnatural car is than figuring out what a natural horse is. Indeed, discussing a car orally or in writing does not require mentally turning its component parts into its original elements of nature. Learning to walk, a biologically hard-wired phenomenon, does not require that we find virgin terrain to do it on. In fact, it is easier to learn to walk on a manufactured flat surface.

How important is it that there are special brain sites where phonological processing occurs? That depends on one's theory of reading. Suppose a supporter of meaning-based reading wanted to study whether the brain had special sites where the observable symbols of oral or written language were utilized. He or she would do exactly what Shaywitz and others have done. Give subjects nonsense words or trigraphs to sound out and run the MRI machine while this is occurring. The MRI will show where the letters are processed. But in such a design no other language cues are available, since the stimuli are not real words and there is no surrounding context other than participating in a study. Thus, identifying brain sites for phonological processing is neutral with respect to the various models of reading. But the value of such information varies with theory. If reading is regarded as the construction of meaning, there is not much interest in what the brain does with nonsense. The conclusion from MRI studies of sounding out letters could then only be that the MRI machine is so powerful it can identify sites of otherwise useless mental gyrations.

Among the more scientifically objectionable and dangerous claims of the phonological processing community is that intensive phonics instruction can repair a dyslexic brain. Before and after MRI pictures of children identified as having difficulty sounding out words, and then given many hours of phonics drills, showed a transformation to the pattern seen in those who were good at sounding out. Authors of the study claimed brain repair. Commentators for *Neurology*, the official journal of the American Academy of Neurology, responded to such a claim by noting that the neuroimaging studies on which the claim is based demonstrate nothing more than the subjects learned how to do something differently than what they had previously been doing (Rosenberger and Rottenberg, 2002). There is absolutely no precedent for claiming that an instructional technique can repair a brain.

Phonological processing advocates cite claims that a region of the temporal lobe is larger in proficient readers than dyslexics. Other brain size differences have been cited. What does this prove? Is it the cause of reading differences or the result? Such discrepancies may exist for exactly the same reason other well-known discrepancies exist. Experienced taxi drivers in London have larger anterior hippocampal regions than matched controls who are not experienced London cabbies. The size difference varies directly with years of experience. This is called *plasticity*. The living brain grows and (shrinks) in response to experience. In other words, the anterior hippocampus grows in response to use in internalizing and developing visuospatial information. Its size remains appropriate for its current demands.

Children who allegedly cannot read also plausibly do not read very much, or certainly not as much as people who do not have such difficulties. Therefore, these brain differences can just as easily reflect this simple difference in the amount of reading that occurs.

Finally there are claims that chromosomes may carry a "dyslexia gene" which places the individual who possesses it at risk for reading problems. This betrays an inherent contradiction. If the brain is, in its fundamental make-up, not hard-wired for written language, that is, not hard-wired for reading, then there can be no specific reading gene. This means that it is highly unlikely for any gene to be specific to dyslexia, and to not manifest itself in some other aspect of cognitive and mental life. A dyslexia-specific gene would have to be a mutation of a non-reading gene that manifests itself only in reading, and, even more, only in phonological processing. But if a mutation of a non-reading gene affects both reading and other psychological phenomena, then this means that there must be potential causes of dyslexia other than an impairment of phonological processing, contradicting the definition of dyslexia that it is a specific impairment of reading not attributable to any other aspects of intelligence, emotion, or physical functioning.

To sum up, in the Shaywitz model of reading meaning, certainly the goal of each linguistic event, makes its appearance only after the automatic processing sequences have been carried out. Meaning does not itself contribute to, or influence, let alone dominate the automaticity of language. It is its final product, not its guiding navigator.

Meaning, or more precisely the real-time construction of meaning, is the foundation of linguistic appropriateness and creativity. It is meaning itself which is the truly novel, creative, and appropriate feature to be found in the contextual application of grammar, belief systems, and knowledge systems. We do not typically create new grammatical rules when using language. We create new meanings.

The issue is, in the end, entirely empirical. What does the evidence tell us about the role of meaning construction in real-time language events? Is it merely the final product in an assembly line sequence of automatic steps? Or is it found earlier in the process, at the outset, guiding the actual selection of automatic processes which certainly do indeed play a role? The transactional socio-psycholinguistic model of reading has made its case based on mountains of empirical data: meaning is present from the very beginning and is constructed more elaborately in the course of a real language event. Meaning controls automaticity, not the other way around.

They have acted as if the only aspect of human psychology that can be studied scientifically is the automatic part, the part that is not subject to whim, to volitional, and deliberate subjective interpretation, in short, to the seemingly uncontrollable. Isn't that the essence of *the* scientific method? Control certain variables in order to study others. But subjective meaning cannot be controlled.

Still, the subjective construction of meaning can be studied because we can identify its manifestations in observable events. Its effects are found in miscues, in eye movement patterns, in the particularities of reportable interpretations. This is the profound contribution of Goodman's model of reading to our understanding not only of reading, not only of human psychology, not only of human nature, but of science as well. And we are now beginning to appreciate how it contributes to our understanding of the operations of the human brain.

A narrow theory of reading, such as the phonological processing theory, is naturally drawn to one of the two main strands in brain research. Specifically, it is attracted to the localizations strand which attempts to identify brain sites that are dedicated to specific functions or representation:

- The occipital region is the site of visual processing.
- The temporal region is the site of auditory processing.
- The left hemisphere is where linguistic elements reside.
- The right hemisphere is where facial recognition occurs.

But another strand of brain research is dedicated to discovering general principles of brain function. So, even though visual and auditory sensory inputs go to distinct sites in the brain, the manner in which the brain transmits the information to more abstract centers is quite parallel.

The psychology that underlies meaning-based theory of reading is more general, more global in its nature than reading per se. Readers construct meaning by formulating semantic predictions that are themselves based on a variety of cuing systems, some more meaning-laden than others. Predictions are confirmed or disconfirmed by incoming text. But making sense of print is an example of making sense of any experience. We make sense of visual scenes, the sounds of nature, and so on. We confirm and disconfirm predictions in reading, looking, and listening.

There can therefore be no one site in the brain where predicting, confirming, and disconfirming occurs. Such psychological events must be a general property of the brain, something built into its overall organization. If we make a linguistic prediction, the brain will activate its special language areas, but if we make a non-linguistic visual or auditory prediction, that must require the same brain processes regardless of the input sources.

## References

Adams, M. J. (1990). *Beginning to read: Thinking and learning about print*. Cambridge, MA: MIT Press.

Destexhe, A. (2000). "Modelling corticothalamic feedback and the gating of the thalamus by the cerebral cortex." *Journal of Physiology-Paris*, 94, 391–410.

Goodman, K. S. (1967). "Reading: A psycholinguistic guessing game." *Journal of the Reading Specialist*, 6(4), 126–135.

Goodman, K. S. and Goodman, Y. M. (1978). *Reading of American children whose language is a stable rural dialect of English or a language other than English*. Washington, DC: National Institute of Education, U.S. Dept. of Health, Education, and Welfare.

Goodman, K. S. and Goodman, Y. M. (2014). *Making sense of learners making sense of written language: The selected works of Kenneth S. Goodman and Yetta M. Goodman*. New York: Routledge.

Hawkins, J. and Blakeslee, S. (2004). *On intelligence*. New York: Times Books.

Lyon, G. R. (1998). "Why reading is not a natural process." *Educational Leadership*, 55(6), 14–18.

Rosenberger P. B. and Rottenberg, D. A. (2002). "Does training change the brain?" *Neurology 58*, 1139–1140.

Shaywitz, S. E. (1996). "Dyslexia." *Scientific American, 275*(5), 98–104.

Shaywitz, S. E. (1998). "Dyslexia." *New England Journal of Medicine, 338*, 307–312.

Shaywitz, S. E. (2003). *Overcoming dyslexia: A new and complete science-based program for reading problems at any level.* New York: A.A. Knopf.

Shaywitz, S., Shaywitz, B., Pugh, K., Skudlarski, P., Fulbright, R., Constable, R.T., Bronen, R. A., et. al. (1996). "The neurobiology of developmental dyslexia as viewed through the lens of functional magnetic resonance imaging technology." In Lyon, G. R. and Rumsey, J. M. (Eds.). *Neuroimaging: A window to the neurological foundations of learning and behavior in children.* Baltimore, MD: Paul H. Brookes.

Sherman, S. M., Guillery, R. W., and Sherman, S. M. (2006). *Exploring the thalamus and its role in cortical function.* Cambridge, MA: MIT Press.

Stanovich, K. E. (1994). "Romance and reality." *Reading Teacher, 47*(4), 280–291.

Strauss, S. L. (2005). *The linguistics, neurology, and politics of phonics: Silent "E" speaks out.* Mahwah, NJ: Lawrence Erlbaum.

Venezky, R. L. (1993). "In search of the meaning of literacy." *Educational Researcher, 22*, 34–36.

Webb, B. (2004). "Neural mechanisms for prediction: Do insects have forward models?" *Trends in Neurosciences, 27*(5), 278–282.

# Making Sense: What We Know about Reading    **4**

We can now say that we have achieved what Edmund Huey (1908) foresaw more than 100 years ago. We have achieved an understanding of the process of reading and in doing so we have managed "to describe very many of the most intricate workings of the mind."

In this chapter, I'll put together what we have learned about the processes and structures of reading. You should already understand why we say that reading isn't a process of seeing and identifying each word in order in what you are reading. Nor is it a simple process of sounding out words. The research that formed the major basis of this understanding utilized miscue analysis, so we'll start with some background.

## Miscue Research: Windows on the Reading Process

### First a General Issue of Perspective

Much of educational research and also psychological research employs a classic experimental model. It involves stating hypotheses, setting up control and treatment groups, and using statistical probability criteria to test the results. This is a well-honored research tradition and it is useful for a number of purposes. Certainly it has been useful in testing new drugs or treatments in medicine. In applying it to language and education, some prior precautions to experimental research often are ignored. In medicine, it is not ethical to try any "treatment" with a new drug or new procedure without investigating the likelihood that it would have some predicted value and not have negative effects. Many suggestions for the treatment of cancer, for example, have no basis in science and would not be permitted on the off chance that they might work.

The experimental research method has sometimes been called "The Scientific Method." It would be more accurate to call it "A Scientific Method." Trial and error is not scientific research. And there is no placebo in language or education. We can't have some kids getting non-education while some get the real education. And there is no way we can control language and language learning. Attempts to control language reduce it to something less than language. Language can be studied in many ways, but when we try to control it so that we can conduct true experiments, we are no longer studying language.

## Miscue Analysis Plus

My research and that of many of my students and colleagues has used miscue analysis and/or two derived methodologies: retrospective miscue analysis and EMMA (eye movement miscue analysis). We've shown you examples of all of these in prior chapters.

Miscue analysis grew out of my earliest research on reading. I had just "discovered" linguistics. In the 1960s when I began my research there was a lot of excitement and controversy over using new linguistic theories to challenge conventional beliefs about virtually all aspects of language.

As a doctoral student at UCLA, I was surprised to find angry arguments— even occasional fist fights—at the National Council of Teachers of English and the Modern Languages Association over grammar, of all things!

## Reading Is a Language Process

"Was anybody looking at reading using linguistic insights?" I wondered. A quick search of the professional literature turned up very few resources. Leonard Bloomfield, a major linguist at the University of Chicago, developed some materials to teach his son (Bloomfield and Barnhart, 1961). Not surprisingly, considering where linguistics was at the time, he produced a kind of linguistic phonics program. Peter's father, Charles Carpenter Fries (CCF), and his mother used descriptive linguistic concepts (Fries, 1963) to teach Peter to read.

Later, in the mid-1960s, C.C. Fries authored a reading book (1966) drawing on contrastive analysis of patterns (it says something about the variation in reading instruction that Peter is still receiving royalties on that program).

Neither program seemed to be the kind of broader application I was looking for. I decided to go into urban schools with a wide range of students and see with my smattering of linguistics if I could describe what kids did when they read (Goodman, 2003). I was at Wayne State University in Detroit and I found a school in Highland Park, an older completely surrounded suburb willing to let me and my two dollars an hour undergraduate research assistant do the study. There were two classes each of first, second, and third grade pupils including within each class, black and white pupils from working class to lower middle class homes. The children lived in the small frame houses most Detroit auto workers owned or rented. The school was near the headquarters of the Chrysler Corporation.

I selected stories from a basal reader series similar to the one in use in the school and chose stories ranging from pre-primer to eighth grade. To get a quick notion of where to start with each child, I made a list of sample words in the stories according to parts of speech (nouns, verbs, adjectives, adverbs, and function words). It is the only time I have ever asked anyone to read words out of context.

I chose every other child on the class list of the six classrooms so I had 100 subjects with about a third in each grade. Though experimental design would not have served my purpose of examining the reading process, without really planning it my design gave me an embedded experiment. I could see whether words not read on the list were read later in the stories. I found an over-whelming effect. Even first graders could read in context two-thirds of the words they had failed to read on the lists. That was not a surprising finding to me or the teachers I shared it with. "We knew that," they said. Curiously, however, several researchers later rejected that finding and tried to prove it was incorrect. It didn't fit their paradigm.

But my own excitement came when I heard a first grader substitute *the* for *a* in reading a story. The children were making substitutions in their reading of words that made sense but were not the ones in the text. They omitted some words and inserted others. They changed word order and shifted clauses from one sentence to the next or vice versa. They were providing me with a rich oral text to compare to the written text they were responding to.

I began to realize that I had found a unique way of peeking into what happened in the head of a reader. By comparing the observed responses (OR) to the expected responses (ER), I could see what the reader was doing in making sense of the text. In no other language situation is such a comparison possible.

I could not call every deviation an error since the responses of the readers were not simply right or wrong. They were produced with exactly the same resources—cues from the text—that produced expected responses. So I called them miscues. And I could use linguistics to compare OR and ER (Goodman, 1969).

In study after study, we developed an increasingly complete way of looking at reading through the actual oral reading of real readers reading real texts. We chose whole stories or articles that were within the interests of our readers and a bit above what was easy for them. We electronically recorded their oral reading. No reader, however proficient, read without some miscues.

Eventually it became clear that reading involves an interaction of thought and language in making sense of any text. That means reading is a psycholinguistic process. We realized the importance of prediction.

It took me a while to realize that miscue analysis is an example of a non-experimental scientific perspective: scientific realism (Goodman, 2008). The goal of the scientific realist is not to look for cause and effect; rather it is to understand the structures and processes of reality. Think of the old tree falling in the forest example used to explain differences between idealists and realists. The scientific realist is concerned with what the difference is between standing and falling trees. What are the processes that keep a tree standing for a hundred years and then knock it down in a strong wind?

Because we look at real acts of reading and work toward a theory of the structures and processes of reading, miscue analysis is scientific realism.

Since miscue analysis always uses real texts, it is easy for classroom teachers to use it informally to get an understanding of their pupils' reading. Further, it is a procedure that can be used in reading of any language. And it is a powerful tool in teacher education to get teachers to revalue their understanding of the reading process.

You can try it yourself. Scan a copy of a short story or an article from a magazine or newspaper. Record yourself or someone else reading the story orally. Then mark down the miscues on the copy you scanned. We use relatively simple transcription techniques.

- Circle omissions.
- Use a carat to show insertions.
- Write substitutions over the words they replace.
- For regressions or corrections, draw a line from where it begins back to where the rereading began.
- Put a small circle with a *c* in it for self-corrections, *uc* for unsuccessful corrections, and *ac* if in the regression a correct reading was abandoned.

Look at the patterns of miscues. You'll quickly see why I can't call the changes readers make errors. Some appear to be alternate ways the author could have written the same meaning. At other times, the reader immediately or at some distance later spontaneously corrects the reading. Always we see some evidence of a reader working at making sense. Do some of the miscues produce acceptable sentences? Are miscues that disrupt meaning corrected? Are there miscues on the same word or phrase that are repeated through the text? When a reader self-corrects, can you see what was predicted? Were there any surprises? How often were substitutions the same part of speech? It isn't necessary to have a complete understanding of miscue analysis to see how rich the information is that it provides. Table 4.1 gives an example of a marked worksheet showing one reader's miscues on a whole story (Goodman, Y. M., 1967).

This worksheet (Table 4.1) shows Franklin's (pseudonym) reading of the first two pages of a primer story.

The book uses the word *toy* for the various items the children in the accompanying pictures are playing with. The only miscues occur on the word *toy* with Franklin substituting the correct noun for each use of *toy:* airplane and train in each case (except where the referent could be either toy).

When asked what the children were doing in the retelling, Franklin said *"They playing with they toys."*

Clearly he knows the word *toy*. And he uses it as a generic term for the group of play items. But he reads the individual word he expects in the text. His rendition is more predictable than the text he is reading.

## Retrospective Miscue Analysis

Retrospective miscue analysis is a logical extension of miscue analysis. It encourages readers to do what you just did: to examine their own miscues. Through this process the readers come to understand that reading is a process of making sense of print. They revalue the process from one of accurate word recognition to one of meaning construction. We've found over the years that many children, adolescents, and even adults have a misunderstanding of their own abilities as readers. To them every miscue, every unfamiliar word is proof that they are poor readers. Helping them to think through their own miscues is often liberating, as they realize that miscues show their strengths and not just weaknesses.

**Table 4.1** Marked Worksheet from Yetta Goodman's Longitudinal Study of Six African American Children

**Franklin**          **April 1966**

|       |                              | marking |
|-------|------------------------------|---------|
| 103   | Here is a little red toy.    | train   |
| 104   | Here is a big blue toy.      | airplane |
| 105   | Come in here for a toy.      | k-   train |
| 201   | Look, Sue.                   |         |
| 202   | Here is a big toy.           | train   |
| 203   | It is a big blue airplane.   |         |
| 204   | And look at the little toy.  | train   |
| 205   | It is a little red train.    |         |
| 206   | Look Here! Look Here!        |         |

## Eye Movement Miscue Analysis (EMMA)

Eric Paulson (2000) made the logical connection of miscue analysis and eye movement research. You've seen how amazing the contrast can be between what the eyes are doing and what the reader is saying in oral reading. Yet Paulson found in looking at the considerable literature of eye-tracking studies that there were few studies of eye movements on complete texts of any length and usually readers were responding to artificial texts created to test hypotheses.

## Quantitative vs. Qualitative

One way to categorize research is whether it is quantitative or qualitative. Experimental research is quantitative. Data is collected, for example, using pre- and post-tests and the degree of improvement is a quantitative measure of improvement of one group over another. Miscue analysis is both qualitative and quantitative. We get a large amount of data on each variable studied— for example, percent of corrected miscues of each type. In a miscue study each reader of a 12 page story may produce 100 or more miscues. Each miscue is examined over as many as 19 variables. There is a huge quantity of data; if we consider each word or punctuation as an opportunity to produce a miscue, the concern for "degrees of freedom," so important in the statistics of experimental research, is meaningless in miscue research.

But we also have qualitative data that tells how the miscues relate to the comprehension of the reader. We're ultimately concerned with the quality of the reading, not simply as an overall measure of competence but also as an indication of the strengths and weaknesses of the reader.

Our measure of comprehension is based on a retelling during an interview with the reader. We also derive a Comprehending Score; it's the miscues per 100 words minus the percent of miscues which were fully acceptable or corrected. Comprehending is a process score: how efficiently was the reader constructing meaning? Comprehension is a product score: how effectively did the reader understand the text being read? Though these scores correlate— comprehension depends on comprehending—the correlation may not be high because what the reader knows before the reading is also a component of how well the text was understood.

The Kenneth and Yetta Goodman Archives at the University of Arizona Library contain all of the data from their studies as well as audiotapes of the reading of each of their many research subjects.

## Learning about the Brain by Studying Reading

When I began my study of reading, my intuition told me that I should ask children read something similar to what they are asked to read in school and see if I could use linguistics to analyze what they were doing. Further, I knew I wanted to have real texts read through by a range of readers typical of an urban population. Very quickly I realized that I had discovered a unique opportunity to study not just what the readers did—but more important— what was going on in the heads of the readers. That's because I could compare their oral responses with the expected responses on the text and what was happening in the text. That is, I could see that their miscues are produced by the same mental processes as their non-miscue responses. So I was not just studying reading. I was studying language processes and I was studying the processes of the brain itself. Miscue analysis gave me a window on the process of making sense of print. And that gave me a window on the way the brain makes sense of everything (see Chapter 3). Huey (1908) had predicted a century earlier what my colleagues and I were realizing: to understand reading is to understand the basic ways in which the brain makes sense of the world because what the brain does in reading had to involve the same structures and processes it uses in all situations. I now perceived that I was a scientific realist looking through a powerful lens at how the brain uses language to construct meaning.

The conclusion of all this miscue research provided a simple answer to the question: what is reading?

## Reading Is a Process of Making Sense of Print

In this simple statement there are some deeper ideas:

### IDEA 1: READING IS A PROCESS BY WHICH THE BRAIN CONSTRUCTS MEANING FROM PRINTED TEXTS

As we have said, the brain uses visual information to construct perceptions. Within our construction of meaning, the brain (specifically the cortex) predicts what the eye will see and constructs mental images based on the visual information but also on the predictions it has made.

It uses these perceptions to construct the wording and other features of the text. And the brain actually constructs a mental text—we call it the reader's text—based on the published text. Remember what you are seeing as you read is not meaning but patterns of ink. You as the reader must construct from them a meaningful text and make sense of it. It is this reader's text which the reader comprehends.

In our research we found it useful to separate in our thinking the process and product of reading. Comprehension is the product—the meaning we have constructed during our reading. Comprehending is the process—the process of meaning making. Comprehension is always the product of two elements: what we knew before we read and what we are able to assimilate or accommodate to enhance and expand on that knowledge.

Comprehending is a dynamic process. Steve described a simple ongoing activity such as reaching for a glass or turning a door knob. He described two elements in how the cortex controls an ongoing process such as a fielder catching a fly ball. The elements are looping and corrective mechanisms. In driving a car in traffic or in reading, a series of decisions are continuously made; each maintains a connection between the cortex, the sensory systems, and the organs of the body. Each decision involves predictions on the basis of percep- tions based on sensory inputs. But they also contain predictions of what is likely to follow.

Consider a few seconds of driving:

> I'm driving in the speed lane but my exit on the freeway is coming up.
> Cortex to foot: keep the foot steady on the accelerator but get ready to change lanes.
> Cortex to eyes / eyes to cortex: check the mirrors for a break in traffic, start turning the wheel—whoa, where did that guy come from? Nice recovery, feet and hands!

Reading is much like that:

> Cortex: message to eyes, eyes to cortex. Ready: hands on page. Initiate reading. Eyes get some input from left of line. Here's what we're looking for: quick focus for a few milliseconds. Thanks eyes: got a hunch of the pattern, predicting, wording, skip ahead now pretty sure what's coming . . . yeah we know what's coming—got the image yeah that's it. Understood! And here's what we're expecting. That's nice input— whoa, eyes go back to the way this began—hold on—nevermind I already know what I missed.

Comprehending is this rapid continuous looping: sensing, thinking, muscle action: cortex makes sense. Occasionally the eye is sent back reversing gears to recheck input and then rolling on.

## IDEA 2: ANY TEXT—WHETHER ORAL OR WRITTEN—IS A COMPLEX SYSTEM OF ABSTRACT SYMBOLS WITH NO INTRINSIC MEANING

And here is the miracle of human language: we are able to think symbolically —that is, use abstract symbols to represent meaning. We connect with each other, communicate our needs, our thoughts, our experiences, our feelings. But there is no meaning in the symbols themselves. The meaning cannot pass from one head to another. It is in the head of the writer who creates the text and the reader who makes sense of the text. And that means, even when the communication is quite successful, the meaning is never a perfect match.

The meaning that we produce is never exactly the meaning the writer had— we all bring our own views and experience into the meaning construction. Poets particularly have understood this. I heard this story from a Canadian professor: once when Robert Frost was speaking to undergraduates at an Ontario University, the professor introducing him expounded in great detail about the meaning of his favorite Frost poem. When finally Frost got up to speak he said, "Then again, it may just be about apple-picking."

## IDEA 3: TO MAKE SENSE OF WHAT IS READ THE READER MUST BRING MEANING TO THE TEXT

Both oral and written language texts have the potential to be understood. But understanding, to any degree, depends on readers bringing meaning to the text. We have it wrong when we say, "Does that make sense to you?" Rather, we should say, "Can you make sense of that?" We don't "get meaning" from the written text, we make our own meaning by using the meaning potential of the text. By that we mean that the writer creates a representation of what he or she means but the writing itself is an array of abstract symbols that has no intrinsic meaning. If the text is well written, a reader who shares the language constructs meaning from it.

Both the reader and the writer are trying to communicate through language. How well they succeed depends on two things:

- that they share the same language, at least substantially enough to understand each other (indeed they may share the same language but use it differently); and
- that the reader brings to the reading the background of knowledge and experience the writer has assumed the intended readers will have. The writer has a sense of audience.

## IDEA 4: MAKING SENSE OF WRITTEN LANGUAGE USES BASICALLY THE SAME PROCESSES AS MAKING SENSE OF ORAL LANGUAGE

Another common illusion is that it is necessary to first turn print into sounds (sound out) and then understand it as we do speech. In this view, written language is not real language but a code for language. But in our extensive research on oral reading miscues we found no evidence for that. In fact, we all read silently much faster than we speak. Rather, the two systems—oral and written language—are parallel. We learn to make sense of each in much the same way. If in fact reading were dependent on turning print to speech then deaf people lacking hearing could not learn to read. Deaf sign languages such as American Sign Language constitute a third parallel language system. The symbols are manual signs and they represent meaning directly just as speech and writing does. Sometimes people talk about "cracking the code" in reading. But language systems are all codes. The symbols have no meaning but in the systematic way they encode meaning.

Of course in listening you make sense of the language as you hear it. If you don't understand something in normal conversation, you can ask the speaker a question. In reading you can reread to get more understanding. In both cases, though, both thought and language are involved.

We use language to represent ideas: whether the input is oral, written, or sign. We construct our own meaning in comprehending what is being said. And we are not limited to speech in how we can connect with each other.

In any case, there is an ongoing transaction in which meaning is expressed in language and comprehended from language. So in reading, the text the reader comprehends is the text the reader is constructing parallel to but not identical to the writer's text. It is no longer just the writer's text, the parallel text is based on what the reader perceives, knows, believes, and understands. So what is comprehended will be a composite of author's and reader's meaning. Exactly the same thing happens in listening. The listener is also constructing a personal text and that is what is comprehended. So when a husband insists that his wife said one thing while his wife insists she said something else, they are both right since what they understood were two different but related texts.

## IDEA 5: HOW WELL ANY READER CAN MAKE SENSE OF ANYTHING THAT IS BEING READ DEPENDS ON HOW EFFICIENT AND EFFECTIVE THE READER IS

An effective reader, like an effective listener, has a good understanding of what is being said. But efficiency is a matter of how much time and energy the reader must expend to make sense.

And here's where you may be surprised: efficient readers use the least amount of time, energy, and cues from the text to make sense of what they are reading. Research has shown for a long time that there is a correlation between the speed of reading and comprehension. That has led to the mistaken notion that if we teach readers to read faster their comprehension would improve. Fortunes have been made from speed reading courses.

However, it isn't speed but efficiency that is related to comprehension. Efficient reading is relatively fast. That's because the reader uses the least amount of cues from the text, selectively, to make sense of what is being read. But proficient reading is always a combination of how efficient the reading is and how effective. Proficient readers are also flexible—they vary the speed at which they read to suit the density or the quality of the text, speeding up when the going is easy and slowing down when they need to use more cues from the text to get to the meaning (even rereading when the reader is unsure of the meaning). And many readers read more slowly or reread when they relish the text they are reading.

Efficiency in reading is also relative. Efficiency requires the least amount of cues necessary based on very effective predictions and effective results. The general admonition of teachers is to read carefully. But reading efficiency will vary depending on the nature of the text, the purposes for reading, and how predictable the text is for the reader. So efficiency and effectiveness are not general attributes but specific to each transaction between a reader and a text.

Each of us is illiterate to some extent. No one is so literate that he or she can understand any text ever written. We read some texts with great efficiency using fewer fixations, sampling the text very effectively, making highly successful predictions. And there are other texts that we have to read ploddingly and repetitiously to get some tentative sense of the meaning. In texts of great interest to us we bring the necessary background to fit ourselves into the intended audience it is written for. When I have to sign an important document such as a mortgage agreement, I get a lawyer to do my reading for me.

## Intuition: Reading as a Psycholinguistic Guessing Game

Albert Einstein has been quoted as saying that all scientific discoveries begin with intuition (Calaprice, 2000). In 1967, when I first claimed that reading is a psycholinguistic guessing game, my claim was such an intuition. Like all intuitions there was some basis to my claim. It had its roots in the experiences I was having studying the miscues children made in oral reading. But a singular event brought me to framing my intuition as a psycholinguistic guessing game.

Early in my career in the mid 1960s, I was invited to spend a month at Cornell University with Project Literacy (Levin and Mitchell, 1969), a federally funded effort headed by Harry Levin, a developmental psychologist. Noam Chomsky, emerging then as the preeminent American linguist, came for three days to work with the small group of about 20 researchers. In his presentation he called reading tentative information processing (Chomsky, 1964). Picking up on the tentative idea, I fit that to my own intuitions. I rephrased that in an article I wrote as a psycholinguistic guessing game (Goodman, K., 1967). By that I meant that the reader is always predicting (guessing what will follow). I had no trouble getting that paper published and it caused a flurry of interest with both negative and positive reactions.

As you did with *The Boat in the Basement* (Gollasch, 1980), I argued that readers sample from the text on the basis of predictions just enough to confirm or disconfirm their predictions. Readers predict what they are about to encounter and then, based on these predictions, sample from the text to confirm or disconfirm them.

Another concept I adapted from Chomsky is the distinction between competence and performance in language (Chomsky, 1965). For him, competence is innate and can be inferred from observing performance. In my adaptation, I consider competence to be continuously developing and the basis for performance. But performance may not always represent competence. For example, an accomplished musician I knew had an automobile accident that made it impossible to perform on his viola. But he still retained his musical competence. He could teach, arrange music, and compose.

In education, our goal is not to change performance but to change competence. In fact, concern for performance in taking a test could result in regurgitation of trivia which is quickly forgotten. In reading, comprehension requires competence. Reading words without comprehension can be the result of instruction that focuses on saying the words rather than understanding the text. In fact the reading process can be short-circuited at several levels ranging from sounding out words to reading accurately without comprehension.

As I began miscue studies with a small grant from Wayne State University, I held a conference on what I ambitiously labeled the Psycholinguistic Nature of the Reading Process. I knew nothing then of Edmund Huey. It seemed that all ten people in the world who were doing anything related to that subject were present. A book with the same name was published out of that conference (Goodman, 1968).

Over the past five decades, we have provided a research base and a more fully reasoned and developed theory that builds on that early intuition. Our understanding of how reading works, as Huey predicted, is consistent with the emerging understanding of how the brain itself works in making sense of the world. As Steve has shown, our model of making sense of print is in every sense an exemplar of how human consciousness works. It can be generalized to a theory of language—since reading is language, what's proven to be true of reading must be true in broad outline of listening. And it goes a long way to providing the basis for a theory of expressive language: speaking and writing.

The intuition we extrapolated from our research about how the brain must be functioning in reading as demonstrated in miscue analysis and EMMA research is now support for the new views of brain function being reported by neurologists and brain theorists.

## Reading Is Cyclical

Reading of course begins with *visual* input: the first thing the reader does is to begin to scan print by moving the eyes across the text. That quickly is followed, however, by a *perceptual* cycle: the *visual* input becomes *perceptual*. Next the reader tentatively makes two simultaneous decisions. What the *grammatical* structure is and what the words are within that structure.

In my earlier models, I called this the *syntactic* cycle as I realized that readers had to decide what the sentence structure or the syntax is in order to get to meaning. But with Peter's help, I understood that perception leads to *wording*. Like the writer, the reader makes grammatical choices at the same time the words are chosen. That's because word forms must fit grammar and grammar must fit word choice. I like Halliday's (2004) term in calling this *wording* (a process). And, of course, what follows then is *meaning*.

So we have the *visual* cycle, the *perceptual* cycle, the *wording* cycle, and the *semantic* (meaning) cycle. But since reading is continuous, each cycle is repeated throughout the reading—it is like a merry-go-round with each cycle following the others but always beginning with *visual* and ending with *meaning*.

## Strategies

What we originally called *psycholinguistic strategies in reading* (Goodman, 1970) we came to understand are the basic strategies of the brain in everything it does. These strategies are as follows:

### INITIATION

Reading is a deliberate act. It starts when we decide there is something to be read. And then our brain swings into action and starts the process of making sense of it. This may seem too obvious to be worth attending to but, on the other hand, it is not automatic. The reader must decide to read and give some selective attention to it and that almost always involves some need or purpose in some context.

### TERMINATION

Again, it may seem obvious that the reader must at some point decide to stop reading. But that also is a conscious strategy. We don't always read from beginning to end. Very often the reader decides at some point to terminate, short of reading to the end of the text. There are any number of reasons: running out of time, finding that it didn't meet the reader's purpose, finding it boring, badly written, not what the reader expected, or having found what the reader was looking for. Typically, for example, we only read, selectively, part way through newspaper articles—just far enough to get the main news but not interested enough to pursue the details. And, of course, some texts such as recipes, directions, and schedules are not meant to be read from beginning to end but rather in short spurts interrupted by actions.

### SAMPLING AND SELECTING

The brain efficiently samples from the input, the eye provides from the text the information it needs in making sense. By sampling, I mean it takes from the visual input what it is seeking to form perceptions. It is selective in that it ignores any visual information that is unrelated to what it is looking for. It uses the eyes, instructing them on where to look and what to look for. As you experienced in reading *The Boat in the Basement* (Gollasch, 1980), the brain is able to suppress some input and focus on what it has anticipated will be useful. It is just as important in listening and reading to know **what not to pay attention to** as it is to know what to pay attention to (two *the's* for example). Remember, the brain controls the eye. And what we think we see is more important than what we actually see.

## PREDICTION AND INFERENCE

What we recognized in our research as central to making sense are the two strategies of prediction and inference. An inference supplies information in constructing meaning implied but not explicit in the text. A prediction is a guess at what may or may not become explicit. These now are being recognized as central to all instances in which the brain is making sense of the world. When I called reading a guessing game, I was not using a metaphor. Predictions are guesses. The more proficient the reader is, the more successful the guesses will be.

In the previous chapter, Steve discusses a feed-forward theory that suggests that each successful prediction carries with it expectations of what will subsequently follow. Peter explains that language is in this sense very redundant. That contributes to both the comprehension and speed of successful reading. No text is ever completely explicit. There is also ambiguity in every text. The reader must infer much of the unstated and / or ambiguous meaning. At any moment in reading, the reader is making new predictions and inferences, tentatively aware that they may need to be modified or rejected.

## CONFIRMING OR DISCONFIRMING

As the loops from cortex to thalamus and back to the cortex operate, readers use the same information to confirm or disconfirm their predictions and inferences as they do to make new ones. A whole genre of predictable books for children learning to read has emerged as our discovery of the importance of prediction came to be understood and accepted by teachers. Predictable books are well written to take advantage of the interests and experiences of young readers. But they have a pattern that repeats itself aiding the reader in anticipating what is coming. *This is the House that Jack Built* (Caldecott, 1878) is a classic example of a predictable story.

## Correction When Needed

Because predictions are informed guesses, readers must always be tentative and ready to reprocess and correct themselves in their reading. There is a continuum between tentativeness and confidence in all reading. That is influenced by the purpose and the context as well as what the reader knows and understands prior to the reading. Miscues that make sense are unlikely to be noticed by the reader unless the reader lacks confidence and shifts from making sense to avoiding errors.

One persistent and logical misconception among teachers of reading is that error is, by nature, bad and ultimately reading should be error-free. Our study of oral reading miscues has demonstrated that reading is never completely without deviations and that miscues result from the nature of reading as a constructive process. Focus on accurate reading is counter-productive since it makes word accuracy more important than comprehension.

Of course the quality of the writing will also contribute to the success of the reader. Putting together a toy following poorly written instructions or trying to use a poorly written computer manual are common examples of comprehension being limited by poorly written texts. Legal texts are difficult for most readers because of the archaic language which has taken on very precise meaning in case law. A phrase such as "due process" for example is a legal term that defines the procedure that must be followed in legal processes because of its use in case law.

## Reading at the Speed of Thought

We used the example earlier of the efficiency of thought processes of hundreds of drivers traveling at high speeds within a few feet of each other on a freeway using their cars as extensions of themselves. They cannot be dependent on their senses to provide information which is then processed to make the split-second decisions. Their brains must be in continuous contact with the senses to supply the sensory input to adjust the predictions that guide the movements of hands and feet that are controlling the car.

Our brains are equally proficient at making sense of language. We can usually make sense of oral language at the speed at which speech is produced, though if the language we are hearing is a second language, we may have trouble keeping up with the speaker. In reading, we make sense even faster since we are not constrained by the slow pace of human speech.

The looping Steve discusses keeps a constant connection between cortex and thalamus and eye so we can adjust to make the continuous choices that ambiguities in the text require—much as the freeway driver adjusts to the high-speed events surrounding the car. The value of letter combinations can change within a single utterance. The same meaning can be expressed by different words or characters and the same words or characters can represent many different meanings in a wide array of configurations. The reader handles it all easily—sampling, predicting, making inferences, speeding up as traffic permits, and slowing down to make corrections, "recalculating," as the disembodied voice of my GPS says.

Language must be systematic for it to work but the systems will always be imperfect and that works just fine. Our brains find order out of ambiguity and use the redundancies that also make language less than perfect to know, in context, which possible values of a given word sequence is the intended one. Our brains deal with this ambiguity through a universal set for ambiguity.

This dynamic, high-speed nature of language processing is central to our understanding of reading but it is hard for many researchers to cope with largely because of research models that require the researcher to keep every aspect of language invariant except the aspect under study. That inevitably destroys the dynamic quality of language and the context that influences it and produces mistaken applications of their findings.

## Universal Reading Process

The process we have discussed above is universal. Reading is much the same in all languages regardless of differences in writing systems. With our Asian colleagues and graduate students we found that for readers of character-based writing the process of reading is much the same as it is in alphabetically written languages (see Goodman, Wang, Iventosch, and Goodman, 2012).

There is a body of research that claims that phonics is used in reading Chinese, but that research is confined to character recognition. Subjects were shown characters out of context and asked to say them. That's like English language reading studies that deal with out-of-context lists of words. There is no way of knowing which sound or meaning relates to a particular Chinese character out of context. When you meet someone at a conference in China or Taiwan, they hold out their name tags as they tell you their names. There is no sure way of knowing which characters represent the particular oral syllables of their names without seeing them.

## The Need for Real Language

It is the use of cues from real texts that make reading efficient and effective. Our brains are efficient at using just enough phonics in the context of the wording—the grammatical and semantic vocabulary choices made simultaneously of a text to construct meaning. That's why it is important that at all stages of development readers must be dealing with real natural texts.

Attempts to simplify texts for learners inevitably make them harder because they lose the natural relationships. So-called decodable books (organized by phonics patterns) are poorly constructed by any criteria. Children taught with such materials were more successful in reading predictable texts than those they were taught with in some recent studies.

The books by Seuss and others to produce easy reading for beginners such as *The Cat in the Hat* (Geisel, 1957) work not because of the wordlists the authors are restricted to use but only because they manage to tell a story in relatively predictable language that keeps the interest of the readers. To really simplify language would take far more knowledge of linguistics than most authors have.

What this brings us to is that books and stories written by professional authors for children to read and enjoy have the characteristics that will make them predictable where word choices and grammatical structures (and patterns of meanings) support each other.

## So Let Me Review What We Have Learned about Reading

Reading is a process of constructing meaning from written texts. The reader transacts with a text and through a text with an author who has created the text to be comprehensible to an intended audience. In the course of this transaction, the reader constructs a parallel text to the text written by the author and it is the reader's text that the reader is comprehending. In doing so, the reader draws on prior knowledge, conceptual schema, and grammatical schema. In the process, the reader either assimilates the information being constructed to existing schemas or accommodates, changing what was known to be consistent with the new information.

Though there is still much to learn, there are no longer any mysteries of the reading process. We have a coherent and comprehensive theory that explains how readers are able to construct meaning or make sense of written texts.

It should not be surprising that our understanding of reading is not yet fully accepted by all researchers. Their belief system strongly influences every aspect of research from the choice of research questions to the design of the means of answering those questions and the interpretation of the results. When Galileo, using the Copernican view of the movement of heavenly bodies, designed his research, it produced a fundamentally new and different set of data and interpretations that contradicted the findings of the existing science of his time. Yet the objects of his study were the same as those of his contemporaries.

What Galileo's adversaries rejected were not the findings of his research but the theory on which it was based and his interpretation of findings in support of the theory. Copernicus himself was so fearful of the response to his theory that he deferred publication until he was on his deathbed. In his book, published in 1543, he said:

> For a long time I reflected on the confusion in the astronomical traditions concerning the derivations of the motion of the spheres of the universe ... The scorn which I had to fear on account of the newness and absurdity of my opinion almost drove me to abandon a work already undertaken.
>
> (Sobel, 1999: 50)

In 1615, Galileo commented on the dilemma of the scientist whose work is rejected by scientists who do not accept the paradigm on which it is based:

> I discovered in the heavens many things that had not been seen before our own age. The novelty of these things, as well as some consequences which followed from them in contradiction to the physical notions held among academic philosophers, stirred up against me no small number of professors—as if I had placed things in the sky with my own hands in order to upset nature and overturn the sciences.
>
> (Sobel, 1999: 67)

I sometimes have been accused of inventing miscues. It took a few centuries for the Catholic Church to pardon Galileo for his heresies. Most people accept his view of the universe though there still is some belief in astrology.

We now understand that comprehension of written language cannot happen any differently than anything else the brain comprehends. Effective and efficient reading is neither more nor less complex than any other mental process. We read, as we do with every other mental activity, with our brains.

And our brains don't sit in the dark waiting for bits of input. They are in control of the senses as much as they are in control of the other organs of the body.

And in spite of the powerful forces in our society that devalue knowledge and promote pseudo-science in place of real science, I have no doubt that our understanding will eventually be accepted and find broad use.

## References

Bloomfield, L. and Barnhart, C. L. (1961). *Let's read: A linguistic approach.* Detroit, MI: Wayne State University.

Calaprice, A. (Ed.). (2000). *The expanded quotable Einstein.* Princeton, NJ: Princeton University.

Caldecott, R. (1878). *The house that Jack built: One of R. Caldecott's picture books.* London: Routledge and Sons.

Chomsky, N. (1964). *Comments for project literacy meeting.* Lecture presented at Project Literacy, Cornell University, August 6, 1964. Chicago, IL.

Chomsky, N. (1965). *Aspects of the theory of syntax.* Cambridge: MIT Press.

Fries, C. C. (1963). *Linguistics and reading.* New York: Holt Rinehart and Winston.

Fries, C. C. (1966). *Merrill linguistic readers.* Columbus, OH: C. E. Merrill Pub. Co.

Geisel, T. S. (1957). *The cat in the hat.* New York: Random House.

Gollasch, F. (1980). *Readers' perceptions in detecting and processing embedded errors in meaningful text* (Doctoral dissertation). Retrieved from ProQuest Dissertations and Theses database. (UMI No. 8107445)

Goodman, K. S. (1967). "Reading: A psycholinguistic guessing game." *Journal of the Reading Specialist, 6*(4), 126–135.

Goodman, K. S. (1968). *The psycholinguistic nature of the reading process.* Detroit, MI: Wayne State University Press.

Goodman, K. S. (1969). "Analysis of oral reading miscues: Applied psycholinguistics." *Reading Research Quarterly, 5*(1), 9–30.

Goodman, K. S. (1970). "Psycholinguistic universals in the reading process." *Journal of Typographic Research, 4*(2), 103–110.

Goodman, K. S. (2003). "A linguistic study of cues and miscues in reading." In Flurkey, A. and Xu, J. (Eds.), *On the revolution of reading: The selected writings of Kenneth S. Goodman* (pp. 117–123). Portsmouth, NH: Heinemann.

Goodman, K. S. (2008). "Miscue analysis as scientific realism." In Flurkey, A., Paulson, E. and Goodman, K. S. (Eds.), *Scientific realism in studies of reading* (pp. 7–21). Mahwah, NJ: Lawrence Erlbaum Associates.

Goodman, K. S., Wang, S., Iventosch, M., and Goodman, Y. M. (Eds.) (2012). *Reading in Asian languages: Making sense of written texts in Chinese, Japanese, and Korean.* New York: Routledge.

Goodman, Y. M. (1967). *A psycholinguistic description of observed oral reading phenomena in selected young beginning readers* (Doctoral dissertation). Retrieved from ProQuest Dissertations and Theses database. (UMI No. 6809961)

Halliday, M. A. K. (2004). "Three aspects of children's language development: Learning language, learning through language, learning about language." In Webster, J. (Ed.), *The language of early childhood. Volume 4 in the collected works of M.A.K. Halliday* (pp. 308–326). New York: Continuum.

Huey, E. B. (1908/1968). *The psychology and pedagogy of reading.* Cambridge, MA: MIT Press.

Levin, H. and Mitchell, J. R. (1969). *Project literacy: Continuing activities.* Washington, DC: U.S. Office of Education, Bureau of Research.

Paulson, E. (2000). *Adult readers' eye movements during the production of oral miscues.* The University of Arizona (Doctoral dissertation). Retrieved from ProQuest Dissertations and Theses database. (UMI No. 9972086)

Sobel, D. (1999). *Galileo's daughter: A historical memoir of science, faith, and love.* New York: Walker & Co.

# Text Features that Help Readers Make Sense 5

We've been talking about how readers—using their brains and their eyes—make sense of what they read. Now we're shifting our focus to the text itself. What is there about the text that makes it possible for the reader to make sense of it?

We're using the word **text** to mean any language unit that can express meaning in some context. Texts have some sort of social—transactional—purpose. They are always embedded in some sort of social transaction. Seeing a text in relation to some relevant social interaction gives the text meaning and makes it comprehensible as a whole. Texts can be as short as a sign beside a road that says "NO PARKING" or "YIELD," or they can be poems or long conversations or novels. A text can be oral or written or sign.

## But Where Is the Meaning?

Let's pause to examine another illusion in reading. As a proficient reader when you read (transact with a text), you are concerned with the meaning which you think you are getting from the text. But all that there is on this page is ink (or simulated ink on the computer display). It is a text only because a writer (and a bunch of editors and printers) put the ink patterns on the page so that you—the reader—could make sense of them.

## The Meaning Conundrum

So here is the conundrum: if there is no meaning in the ink patterns then in what sense is the text "meaningful?" The meaning is never in the printed text. But the text is created by the writer to represent meaning and you and the writer share control of the system sufficiently that you can (and here are those words again) *make sense.* Where is the meaning? It's in the writer and the reader. The text only has the potential to be understood. This is true of both oral and written texts.

Let's be honest: the patterns of ink aren't just random scratchings. They're signs—abstract units of a symbol system. They differ from each other in at least one way so that they can have a value in the company of other signs. Let's go one step further—you can't really make sense of my text as the writer. As was said in the previous chapter, you create your own text using the same rules (more or less) as I did to create mine. And it is that text that you are making sense of. And how do the two texts differ? You bring to the reading your knowledge, beliefs, and relevant experience. If I've done a good job as the writer, and I have a good sense of my audience, that should make your job easier. If you do a good job as a reader—you have to be trying to make sense—and if you have a good sense of what I am writing about—then our meanings will be similar. But the text you construct and the sense you make of it is yours, not mine. There will always be minor or major differences in what I thought I was saying and what you have come to understand, depending on how much we already share in knowledge and beliefs.

## Reader Response Theory

Literary critic Louise Rosenblatt (1978) approaches meaning from the vantage of reader response theory. For a long time, literary critics believed meaning resided in the text. From that perspective, the reader must uncover the author's meaning. Rosenblatt took the view that meaning is in the response of the reader to the text. She built on John Dewey's (Dewey and Bentley, 1949) concept that there is a transaction between the knower and the known in which each is changed. That fits with our view that a parallel text is constructed by the reader. The change in the reader is the accommodation to the meaning the reader is constructing.

## Systems of Language

 As literate users of English, you and I control its systems. We learn the systems of language early in life as the means of connecting with our families and the others we depend upon. There would be little communication if we didn't. The system is complex. It has to be complex to express the full range of meanings we need to express.

Every human from birth has the ability in social contexts to create language. Language is always used in a personal/social context and always requires a creative contribution from the language user. In other words, texts and language in context are not mere hierarchies of grammatically generated structures that are processed automatically. Language is the way humans connect with each other and it changes its nature in the real world of time and space.

You might ask where did these complexities come from? They were created by people—not in the sense that someone designed and invented language. Rather they were invented in a personal-social process over time as individuals sought to connect with each other. Every one of us has the ability to create language and we continue to do so. The current form of a language is the product of centuries of this process of personal-social invention.

You have only to listen to an old movie to realize that some aspects of language change rapidly—mostly the wordings we prefer—while the more systematic aspects of language seem to change more slowly.

Written language is parallel to oral language (for people who can hear). The wording of oral English and written English are generally the same and so is the grammar. I say generally because the contexts in which each is used requires different wordings and different grammatical structures. Written language is somewhat more resistant to change than oral, particularly when it is used in more formal contexts. The grammar of oral language is actually somewhat more complex because intonation helps to make the complexities more comprehensible.

## Text Structure

Meaningful texts are not only sets of words or sequences of sentences. Whether oral or written, a text must have a structure. And the structure has rules for how it may or may not be used. But these rules and structures develop in the context of their use. There are only so many ways that the human vocal apparatus can vary sounds, shift from one sound to another, and then, too, how the human ear can discriminate between different sounds heard in rapid order. There are only so many ways graphic shapes can be sequenced, arranged, and produced with optimal effort.

To convey a simple experience, there must be ways of indicating who did what to whom or to what, or ways to indicate the topic and what is said about it. The choice of symbols used is one constraint on the system of any language. And so is the context of their use.

People tolerate more variability in oral language just because it is usually being composed as we utter it. On the other hand, we expect more consistency in written language because the writer can edit it before it gets to the reader.

Please understand that by admitting that language—oral, written, or sign—has no intrinsic meaning, we are not saying that texts cannot be beautifully constructed, pleasing to the ear or eye-worthy of a prize, or of being learned by heart. But these are due to the ability of the author to use the system to construct a text so well put together that it evokes responses from its intended readers.

## How Texts Convey Meaning

With this amount of theory in mind, let's look at written texts to see how they are put together to convey meaning. But as we show how language works, keep in mind that almost all people are able to learn one or more languages well enough to communicate what they need to their caregivers by the time they're three or four years old. As complex as language appears, it works for its users and it is not hard for young humans—or old ones for that matter—to learn.

When we talk about how the systems of language work, we're not talking about school subjects, we're talking

**Matching How the Brain Works**
There is another important constraint on how language develops. It must fit the way the brain itself works—the way it uses systems of abstract signs to represent in thought the sense it makes of the world. It is easy for very young children to learn because it fits the way their brains work.

about aspects of language every user must know for it to work. There is no language that lacks grammar. We may learn some of the niceties of language (sometimes called "usage") in school but we learn its grammar as we learn to talk and understand speech.

Every use of oral language is a speech act. Think of every time you read or write as a literacy act. A literacy act is always in some social context. Physical acts—such as opening or closing doors, turning lights off and on, exchanging goods for money, gestures, eye contact, and so forth are also involved. Think of how much of a play or a movie is in the actual dialog and how much more is in the actions and scenes that frame the dialog. It is also important to remember that language does not operate separately, but is always used in some social context to achieve some social goals. This social transaction forms another layer that is outside language but is intimately related to what is said and how it is interpreted.

## Three Levels of Language and their Systems

Language itself has three levels or strata, each with its separate system: the system of symbols (sounds or graphic forms), the system of words and grammar, and the system of meanings. The technical terms for these three systems are the sign system (phonological or orthographic), the lexico-grammatical (wording) system, and the semantic system.

It's convenient to discuss each level of language—and its system—separately so that we understand the workings of the system, but they do not exist in any sense separate from each other and they are used simultaneously. They work for us and they are shaped by the ways they are used. And perhaps they work *because* they fit the way our brains work.

The only observable aspect of language—what we can see or hear—is the sign level. Even at this *observable* level, the elements are really only representations of abstract units. If you were to write the sentence you are reading now, what you wrote would look very different than the print you are reading. Yet someone else would be able to read it as if it were the same. Words are represented by sounds or the letters. But, sounds or letters are not words: in a certain pattern they cue the wording. *Card* contains the same sequence of sounds as *car*, but does not involve the *car*. The written letter sequence *c a r* is linked to some meaning or set of meanings (automobile, railroad car). But the reader or listener must make the connections to the wording and make sense of language. When we are communicating through language, we are usually less interested in the words and grammar that are used than we are in the meanings that are expressed through those words and grammar. But we have to use them to get to the meaning.

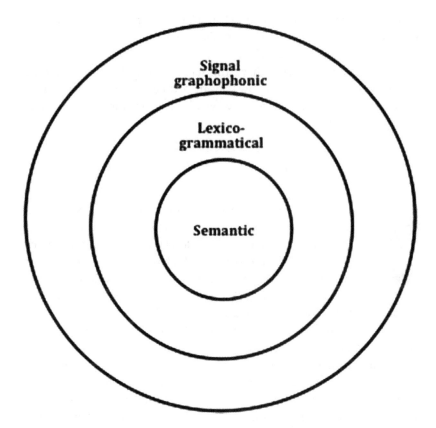

**Figure 5.1** Levels of Language

We've represented the three levels of language as a set of concentric circles, with phonology (what we hear) and orthography (what we see) being at the outside since it can be observed directly, and semantics on the inside, since we have to use the outer systems to get to the meaning. In reading we use the term graphophonics in alphabetic systems to include the orthography and phonics which is the relationship of orthography to phonology that readers would be using.

When there is effective comprehension, we have the illusion that the outer layers aren't there. This has always frustrated linguists. Every competent language speaker seems to know well what is needed to use the language effectively but no one has yet produced a full grammar that deals with all of the language intricacies. In fact, a respected manner of studying language is introspection. Linguists say to themselves what is acceptable and what is not and then examine their own judgments. Or, if they are studying an unfamiliar language, they ask a native speaker.

Ordinarily, language users have the sense of directly communicating meaning with no awareness of how they are getting to it. But if they hear or see a language they don't know, they even have a hard time distinguishing the sounds or letters.

## The Whole and the Parts

The three language layers we just described can also be seen, from the reader's or listener's perspective, as a set of cuing systems, with the cues at each level providing information that may be used to recognize and interpret structures and units at the other levels. The reader is using cues from all three strata at the same time. What is visible is the print, but as we read, the brain uses its knowledge of language to organize how it processes the print. It assigns grammatical structures and makes word choices and does this all as it seeks to construct meaning.

What differentiates a text from a set of words or even sentences is that it is structured to convey a unified meaning in some social context. We have to look at the whole text as a unit of language that has the potential to convey meaning and connect the author to the reader. *Exit* is a text when it hangs over a door, so is a sign with an arrow that says *This way out*.

The purpose of all language—written, oral, or sign—is to connect with others and communicate meaning. In looking at how written texts are organized to make that possible, we'll start with how the meaning is organized, then move to how the wording—the grammar and word choices—are organized in texts. Then we'll examine how the orthography—the graphic system—works. The purpose of all written, oral, or sign is to express meaning in ways that can be understood by others.

The reader is always moving toward meaning and does not need to fully process each level to get to the next. In this sense, there is a difference between

reading and writing. The writer must produce a representation of meaning complete enough for the reader to make sense of it. In making sense, the reader moves as efficiently as possible to meaning.

*Freddie Miller, Scientist* (Moore, 1965), adapted for a basal reading program, will provide a good vehicle for our purpose to see how text is conveying meaning. For convenience we'll refer to the story as FM each time we cite it. We are going to analyze the story in the way a linguist might. No reader needs to analyze a story in this way to understand it or read it (though they cannot construct meaning without using text features) but it helps us explore what makes the text comprehensible.

Here are the first ten sentences of this story:

"What queer experiment" is an example of how wordings change and meanings migrate. No current writer would have chosen this wording.

1. Poor Freddie was in trouble again.
2. He had been experimenting with his chemistry set, and Elizabeth's doll had turned green.
3. His little sister was heartbroken.
4. Freddie's mother was angry.
5. "You've wrecked that doll!" she exclaimed.
6. "What queer experiment was it this time?"
7. "I was only washing the doll to make it look like new," Freddie explained.
8. "I made a special mixture."
9. "But I guess I added too many chemicals to the mixture."
10. "I guess you did," Mrs. Miller said.

What's the difference between this group of sentences and a collection of sentences gathered from several different texts or a set of unconnected sentences?

Of course, a reader could view these ten sentences as a set of unrelated sentences. One critical difference lies in what readers bring to the page and how they perceive it. The several features that distinguish this text and all texts from mere collections of sentences can be grouped under two headings:

1. The structure of the text as a whole. There is an underlying structure that carries the storyline and makes it a text.
2. The links that relate the meanings expressed in each clause. The elements that carry the story are linked across the text.

Every sentence consists of one or more clauses. A clause is a unit of language that can represent meaning. What is important about texts is that they represent related meanings which unify the text.

## Kinds of Meaning

Louise Rosenblatt (1978) says that the meaning may be *efferent*—the factual kind of meaning and/or *aesthetic*—the feelings the meaning represents. Michael Halliday (2004b), as a linguist analyzing texts, sees three kinds of meaning. It is *experiential*—what is happening and what concepts are being expressed, or it is *interpersonal*—the social feelings and relationships the text is conveying. He adds a third type of meaning: *textual*—how the structure of the text itself relates meaning.

Rosenblatt's efferent reader is seeking the experiential meaning while her aesthetic reader is more interested in the interpersonal.

In Halliday's view (2004b), every clause expresses all three types of meaning at the same time.

### Experiential Meaning

This shows some aspect of a real or fictional world. Many clauses describe what something or someone did. For example, I *made a special mixture* tells us what Freddie did. *The doll turned green* is also an example.

### Interpersonal Meaning

*Poor Freddie* is not describing Freddie as poor (without wealth); rather Freddie is to be pitied by the reader. His sister was clearly upset. But *heart-broken* is interpersonal—an opinion of the narrator expressing how deeply upset she was. Interpersonal meanings convey feelings or attitudes to the reader/listener. Interpersonal meanings also include any indications in the language of the speaker's relative social position. For example, statements, questions, and commands all differ in the way they position the writer/speaker with respect to the reader/listener.

*You've wrecked that doll!* is less a fact than an attitude. *Wrecked* is a pretty strong term for what happened. *Queer* is not an attribute of experiments; it shows rather the mother's view of her son's experiments. As the child, Freddie may not express similar views of her without getting in serious trouble. In the conversation between Freddie and Mrs. Miller, in the passage above, we see Mrs. Miller primarily expressing how she feels. Freddie offers a weak defense: *I was **only** . . .* That word *only* is his attempt to diminish his offense. It wasn't a *queer* experiment because he had a noble motive: to *make the doll look like new.*

## TEXTUAL MEANING

Textual meaning occurs where the text structure itself has meaning potential. The use of alternate fonts such as bold or italics to differentiate meaning would be an example of textual meaning.

## Generic Structure

Different genres have relatively fixed sequence of elements (for example, recipes and articles in scientific journals). The nature of the genre task limits the structure and the language used in it.

Consider what the author has accomplished in the opening we read. She's introduced the three main characters, Freddie Miller, his "little" sister Elizabeth, and Mrs. Miller, their mother. She's presented the central problem of the story: Freddie does chemistry experiments that cause problems. And we know a bit about the three characters and how they relate to each other, particularly the tension between mother and son. That's quite a lot to achieve in this brief opening. And, of course, she achieved her main goal: to capture the interest of her readers in wanting to know how the problem will be resolved.

For contrast, here's the opening of another story, *Poison* by Roald Dahl (1958), we've used in our research. We'll cite it henceforth as (P).

> It must have been around midnight when I drove home, and as I approached the gates of the bungalow I switched off the headlamps of the car so the beam wouldn't swing in through the window of the side bedroom and wake Harry Pope.

The task here is somewhat different. There is a strong sense of time and place. And there is a tension which will become a theme of the story. The two characters are introduced, though the first-person narrator is so far unnamed. And the reader is set up to wonder about their relationship. Even the experiential meaning is somehow intriguing—what kind of a bungalow has gates and why did it say headlamps? And notice here that the author has chosen to accomplish this with a single complex sentence.

(FM) has a structure that is predictable for anyone who knows books written for children. Modern children learn to expect this structure from digital texts, TV, films, and so forth as well as from reading and hearing stories told. Freddie, the main character, likes to experiment and fix things. However, his efforts often turn out wrong. The story begins with the other characters upset at Freddie because he attempted to clean a doll—but it turned green. After two more episodes that have similar results, he helps his sister who is stuck in a closet, and everyone is very happy and proud of Freddie.

What the reader knows from the opening (placement) is reinforced in the subsequent episodes. We know how his mother and sister feel about Freddie's experiments which moves now from criticism to punishment. Each of the following episodes consists of at least two parts: the first part describes what Freddie did, and the second describes how the other characters react to his actions. The characters' evaluations are prominent in this story, and an important aspect of this story is the fact that these evaluations change.

The narrator often describes Freddie's thoughts and reactions directly, while the thoughts and reactions of the other characters are described only by the characters themselves.

*Sometimes <u>he thought</u> that a scientist's life was filled with disappointments. But <u>he</u> still <u>thought</u> it more fun to pretend to be a great scientist, mixing the strange and the unknown.*

*"I'll keep this for a while," <u>he thought</u> <u>happily</u>.*

There is also the sub-theme of evaluation with Freddie being compared to his uncles:

**Freddie had heard a lot about Uncle August, and a lot about his other uncles too.**

(P) has a different structure representative of Dahl's (1953) adult short stories:

- opening: narrator arrives home being careful not to wake Harry Pope

 I used the story *Poison* in my classes for many years before I fully understood it. That's because of the use of the word *bungalow* as a name for a dwelling. I was aware that the setting is India and even knew *bungalow* was actually a Hindi word.

But not until an Indian graduate student informed my class what the *bungalow* means in India did I fully understand. Unlike the small cottage or cabin I and my North American students visualized, in India a *bungalow* is a very substantial house (hence the gates) and in colonial times in India, Harry and Timber would have been British colonial officials in such a house. That, of course, makes their reaction to the local Hindu doctor much more significant. My purpose in telling this story is once again to emphasize that making sense of a text depends on what the reader brings to the text.

- notices Harry's light is on
- enters house and proceeds to Harry's room
- Harry informs narrator (now identified as Timber Wood) that while reading a small deadly snake slid under the sheets and is now (he believes) asleep on Harry's abdomen
- decision to call local Hindu doctor
- explore solutions
- doctor decides to soak mattress in ether
- careful insertion of tube to insert ether very tense
- sheet is removed
- surprise ending gives new meaning to title
- this also is highly predicable for short story readers and particularly for those familiar with the author (known for his surprise endings).

Clearly, story structures, like all genres, are embedded in the cultures in which they are produced. (FM) is the typical story for children with a happy ending.

## Registers

We call the varieties of language that are used in different social situations *registers*. The different social contexts strongly determine the choice of terms, relative formality or informality, as does the writer's sense of audience—who are the intended readers and what will they bring to the text? Features of register in the text are also more than a sequence of events or episodes. There are threads that run through the text that unify the whole—that give cohesion.

## Cohesion and Cohesive Ties

For example, we see several pronouns sprinkled through the (FM) passage: *he*, *his*, *you*, and *she*. These pronouns are special words in that they maintain reference to someone or something across the text and tie it together. My rule of text writing is: always use a pronoun except when you can't. You can't when (1) what it replaces has not occurred or (2) when the referent would be ambiguous.

Another way to create cohesive ties—to link portions of a text together— is to repeat words or chains of related words. We see *doll* in sentence two and again in sentence five (see page 87). That repetition creates a link between those two sentences. Similarly the occurrence of *experimenting* in sentence two and of *experiment* in sentence six, despite the fact that one instance is a verb and the other a noun, creates a cohesive tie between sentences two and six.

Most texts contain many words that have similar meanings. For example, our passage contains a number of verbs of saying: *exclaimed, explained,* and *said.* Though these are not repetitions of the same word, they all express related meanings and so tie the text together.

Some examples in (FM):

| | |
|---|---|
| *mother, sister, father, parents, uncle, husband, brother* | [family members] |
| *told, called, exclaimed, explained, said, saying, thought, asked* | [associated with verbal processes] |
| *shouted, reply, replied, answered, wanted to know, smiled* | [quotations] |
| *added, taped, ran* | [he *ran* the wire up the sides of the two batteries to the bulb] |
| *winding, placed, got* | [verbs of placement] |

Some of these chains are references to the same entities in several clauses. These are identity chains. In the opening sequence above, all but one sentence contains at least one reference to Freddie. That set of references to Freddie constitutes an identity chain. Three other, shorter identity chains consist of references to Freddie's mother, to his sister, and to the mixture Freddie created.

A second sort of chain consists of words of similar meaning when they occur in related contexts. The verbs in the context of saying—*exclaimed* (5), *explained* (7) and *said* (10) (see numbered sentences p. 87)—constitute such a chain. In writing English, authors avoid repeating the same word so they use synonyms or alternate ways of saying the same thing, so these chains are quite common.

Another sort of cohesive tie is established by relations among the various sentences and clauses of the text. Dialog is a conversational chain involving turn-taking by the participants.

Although the grammar of dialog is complex, most readers find it easy to read because its structure is similar to the structures of spoken dialog they already use in daily speech.

Relations that draw from logical and rhetorical relations can be signaled by conjunctions. *I was only trying . . . but I guess I . . .*

Sometimes two sentences may be placed together for the reader to infer a conjunctive relation. The passage below from (FM) illustrates this situation:

> *He ran to the cellar and picked up the small battery he had intended to use for his mother's bell.*
>
> *In his tool box he found another battery, a ruler, a coil of copper wire, a small bulb, and tape.*
>
> *Carefully he taped the batteries end to end on the ruler so that they touched.*

No conjunction or adverb expresses a relation among these sentences and yet readers interpret these three sentences as narrating a sequence of actions performed by Freddie in the order in which they are presented in the text. Young readers frequently remember this sequence almost verbatim.

So the story has a semantic structure. To tell the story, the writer creates grammatical structures to frame the words that will express the meaning. And the reader must also assign grammatical structures to frame the words to construct meaning. In our research, the reader's intonation in oral reading was a strong indicator of which grammatical structure the reader was assuming.

One sentence in the (FM) text produced miscues that illustrated the importance of listening for intonation:

> *But he still thought it more fun to pretend to be a great scientist, mixing the strange and the unknown.*

In this sentence, the readers expect a noun to follow the adjectives *strange* and *unknown*. But there is no noun and their voices hang on a high pitch on the adjectives showing they expected a noun.

In the discussion above, we mentioned chains of references to a single entity such as (FM) and we have mentioned chains of words of similar meaning. We can examine the clauses of the text to see how those chains interact. For example, in the last episode of (FM), Freddie has decided to build a light for his sister to keep her calm.

- At once Freddie set to work seriously at something [[he had started for fun]].*
- He ran to the cellar and picked up the small battery [[he had intended to use for his mother's bell]].

- In his tool box he found another battery, a ruler, a coil of copper wire, a small bulb, and tape.
- Carefully he taped the batteries end to end on the ruler [[so that they touched]].
- He taped the wire tight across the bottom of the end battery.
- Then he ran the wire up the sides of the two batteries to the bulb.
- After winding the wire around the bottom of the bulb, | | he taped it in place.*
- Next he placed the bulb [[so that it touched the cap on the top battery]].
- The bulb began to glow!
- Freddie taped the bulb in place on the ruler.
- Now he had a homemade flashlight for Elizabeth.
- He tied a string around the end of the ruler | | and hurried back upstairs.

* Clauses are marked off by [[ ]] or separated by | |.

There are many parallels among these sentences. All but one of the main clauses have Freddie as subject. They describe things that Freddie put on the ruler in sequential order. So this group of clauses constitutes a kind of unifying element in which each clause is interpreted by how it relates to the meanings of the other clauses.

## The Nature of Genre Texts

So far what we've explored is one kind of text—narrative. Every genre of text has a structure that relates to what it is used for. Each genre will have some variation of an overall structure that makes it comprehensible.

The beginning lets the reader know what kind of text it is and what will happen. Then there will be a sequence of events, a series of expositions, and presentation of "facts." And then there will be a conclusion that ties the pieces together and returns to the purpose.

We've dealt here with how the overall meaning is represented. In the next chapter, we'll investigate what Halliday calls the lexicogrammar of language (2004a).

### Order and Disorder

There is considerable order in language but there is also disorder. No human language is perfect. I hope we have convinced you about the need for order, for language to be systematic. But why is there so much disorder or irregularity in language? Why *isn't* language perfect? The ancient Greeks had an answer: the gods made language so it had to be perfect. But people misused and corrupted it.

Why in every language does the same word have many meanings and why are there so many ways of saying the same thing? Why are there homophones, homographs, and homonyms? Language is constantly changing but as language communities become more sophisticated, knowledgeable, and educated, shouldn't the change be toward a more perfect form? Shouldn't language become more regular and simpler as it matures and changes? Why do strange phenomena such as the many different forms of BE—*is, am, was, were, be, been, being*—persist? Why do some languages lose future tense or second-person plural? If alphabetic writing is the end product of evolution, why do non-alphabetic forms of writing continue in use? And why is language perception so clearly based on illusion?

Though language is governed by rules, many rules have exceptions. There are two major reasons that language is imperfect:

1.  It needs to be. If it were perfect, it would not serve our needs.
2.  It can be. By that I mean that our brains are comfortable with all this imperfection. Not only can our brains make sense of imperfect language, they thrive on it. Our brains are equipped with a set for ambiguity. They make excellent use of redundancy. Something in the way the human brain uses language handles the imperfections within the systems, so language can be malleable, flexible, and recursive. The Greeks were wrong about the origin of language but right about why it is imperfect. People make it that way.

## The Universal Need for Change in Language

If language were perfect, its many users would need to use it in exactly the same way. And that would require that each of its users would have to rather quickly move toward mastery of the perfect form.

But that would also mean that language would be unchangeable. And change is, in reality, one of the few agreed upon universal characteristics of language. It changes by generation in the same family or community; it changes as people move apart over distance or interest or perspective. And it changes because what we need it for changes.

Much language change comes from our increasing need as a species to connect as society becomes more complex. That brings new functions for language and new technologies to achieve them which, in turn, makes more functions possible. As individuals, we change the way we use language as we join new communities, interest groups, or occupations. We add dialects or registers as we need them.

But some change comes simply because all of us have the ability to create language. We don't always know how the language is usually used to express thoughts new to us so we invent ways of saying what we need to say. A lot of this new language stays within the group that invents it but with mass media it can also spread rapidly or it can fall into disuse and become outdated—like the dialog in old movies.

## The Universal Ability of Thinking Symbolically

Our human ability to think symbolically, to represent our thoughts and meanings with meaningless symbols that stand for meaning, is totally recursive, and it has to be, otherwise it would be limited in how we could use it. Symbols not only can represent meaning—they can also represent other symbols and they can change what they represent within the same context. Look at all the lines and curves that I am using to represent in print what I am trying to say. Chinese has many characters but they are composed of only eight different strokes.

## Our Language Is also Different Depending on Who We're with and Our Purpose

Remember, language is used as a means of transacting with others. The social interaction both limits the sorts of meanings being expressed and provides a means of interpreting what gets said. Social transactions vary in their nature depending on the following factors:

- What social activity is taking place?
  For example: a lecture on physics, or a group of physics students cooperating in a lab, or a group of researchers discussing the latest results of their experiments, or a novel that has scenes that describe several scientists interacting.
- What are the social relations among the participants?
  Are they peers? Teachers and learners? Authors and readers?

How well do the participants know one another?
- What is the role of language in the transaction?
Is the primary medium a lecture? Or does it accompany a physical action as in cooking or playing a game or assembling a toy? Is it the screenplay for a film?

## Ambiguity and Redundancy: Order in Disorder

What often puzzles people as they think about their own language is that on the one hand it is often ambiguous—shouldn't it be more precise? And on the other hand it is so redundant. Shouldn't a communication system be mean and lean with each bit of information represented once and once only? Though these different but related aspects of language would seem to make the language more difficult to use, language would not work at all without them. As we explore them you'll get some insights into how our brains use language to think, learn, and communicate.

### LANGUAGE IS PERVASIVELY AMBIGUOUS

Philosophers have regularly worried that the language we use every day is ambiguous—indeed, pervasively ambiguous. Some philosophers have even developed languages (for example, mathematical logic) that do not have the ambiguity of normal everyday language. But even though we often get into trouble because the language we use is ambiguous, we could not use it effectively for our needs without that very ambiguity. Here are reasons why language is profoundly ambiguous:

**Reason 1:** Language Is a Semiotic System—A System of Meanings that Are Expressed by Words and Constructions in Context

No linguistic form (word or structure) is inherently meaningful. Every word or sentence we use gains its meaning from the way we use it. As the conventions for use change, the meanings change. Thus *nice* used to mean "foolish/stupid." *Silly* (etymologically related to German *selig* "holy/sacred") was first used to mean "deserving of compassion" and "helpless, defenseless." Think of the modern uses of words like *hot* and *cool*, which were originally temperature words but now have taken on quite different meanings.

These changes in meanings are the summations of trends in the individual uses that words are put to. Rarely do we coin brand new words to express new ideas. Much more commonly we extend the use of existing words, by metaphor or by abduction—transferring a meaning from one context to another—like sharp moving from a cutting edge to a musical term to a way of dressing.

Or we create terms by analogy: after the Watergate scandal, called that because of the hotel it occurred in, named for a gate at the Tower of London, future scandals had "gate" tagged on to them.

In other words, every time we use a word we shape its meaning slightly. So, for example, in modern English we use the word *virus*. The earliest use of this word that is documented in the OED dates from 1599 and refers to venom as produced by a poisonous animal. The earliest English usage of *virus* to refer to an infectious organism dates from 1881. Of course it is natural that an adjectival form *viral* would be invented and one appears first in 1948 in phrases such as *viral agents* and *viral hepatitis type A*.

Since the development of computers, a new use of *virus* has become common; we often refer to computer viruses. And recently a new use of the adjective *viral* has developed (too new to be included in my digital version of the OED) in which YouTube clips and blogs are said to *go viral*.

Whether we like these new developments or not, these changes are a natural part of language being used by many people to stretch or to represent new experiences or changing social attitudes. Of course since the changes are gradual, and further, because the older meanings do not automatically disappear as the new usages develop, every word is, to some extent, ambiguous. And of course there is a generational difference in whether we accept or reject the shifting language.

Related to the search for new ways to express familiar ideas is the notion that ways of talking may come to be viewed as worn out and old-fashioned or inappropriate for some other reason (such as avoiding old sexist uses of language). What we call slang typically originates as an effort on the part of some subgroup of society to create new, distinctive ways of saying familiar things. However when slang terms move into general use in the larger community, they are often abandoned by the subgroup that originated them because they are no longer distinctive. Teens, minorities, musicians give terms new meanings and then move on to new ones when other groups adopt them. Some current slang finds permanency and general use. What Americans call sweaters started out as a slang term for a garment that made you sweat similar to a sweat shirt. But then it lost its connection to sweat and became a wide range of knit garments.

Words can also be borrowed from other languages. American English is peppered with terms like *cookie, rodeo, chutzpah, pasta, liverwurst, pate,* and *sputnik.*

English, with its roots in both German and Romance languages, has a system of Latin-based words such as *construct, disembark,* and *prepare* using prefixes and bases that is used in more formal situations, and a more open system of verb plus particles such as *build up, get out,* and *make out.* Think of the many meanings of *make-up.*

**Reason 2:** Any Language Is also Ambiguous Because, as We Said, the Wide Range of People Who Use it Can't Use it in Exactly the Same Way

Every individual has the universal ability to invent language. Every group is using language in special ways to serve their own needs. A teenager once told me he was painting his car "candy apple green." Candy apple was his term for iridescent.

**Reason 3:** Our Ability to Think Symbolically

Perhaps the most important reason for so much ambiguity in language goes back to what makes human language possible. Signs represent reality but they can represent other signs. Every language user has a set for ambiguity: given the particular context we can disambiguate for ourselves the ambiguities from shifting representations.

In our alphabetic writing, it doesn't bother us that lines and circles take on different significance. We can let the orientation of a line and ball be significant in telling a *b* from a *d* or make directionality significant in telling a 6 from a 9. But Chinese can be written from left to right, right to left, or top to bottom. In the Roman alphabet, a single vertical line can be a capital I or a Roman numeral I or a part of a T, E, F, etc.

There is, of course, a limit on ambiguity in language. Too much ambiguity would make communication less successful. Cursive writing is easier for most people to write than manuscript (printing separate letters) because it flows with fewer interruptions. But each person's handwriting is unique. And often letter parts are left out or obscure. That creates a level of ambiguity which can interfere with comprehensibility. If the handwriting is too deviant— the shapes too ambiguous—it becomes difficult to comprehend. In this electronic digital age, the utility of cursive writing—its speed and flow—has been replaced by texting and computer fonts and so cursive writing is being rapidly abandoned by young people.

Consider the array of different fonts available on today's computer and printer. We find use of different fonts for different language functions useful. A wedding invitation would use more ornate fonts while a utility bill would look strange in such fonts. Newspapers make use of special fonts for special purposes but rely on a singular distinctive font that makes it recognizable to its viewers. In any language, the letters or characters can take on an amazing variety and still be read successfully. Again, this is because of our set for ambiguity. We perceive quite varied forms as variations of a single abstract entity. There is no single form for a, b, or c, etc. But our brains perceive them as if the different forms of each letter were the same.

## REDUNDANCY: REDUCTION OF UNCERTAINTY

In Chapter 2, Peter discussed redundancy in language. Speakers and writers want to be understood by their intended audiences. They do so by providing redundant devices in their language choices. In oral conversation, it's common to cycle back to something already said to make sure it was understood. This is one kind of redundancy in language.

But language itself is profoundly redundant. One obvious type is where the same information is conveyed in multiple cues. Here's a simple example: _Those_ boys _were_ asking _their_ teacher some good questions. Subject-verb agreement is an example of redundancy. In Spanish the shift from singular to plural requires multiple consistent shifts: _La mariposa monarca_ becomes _las mariposas monarcas_.

All parts of grammatical patterns provide information that can be used to recognize and interpret other parts of the pattern. Choosing _boys_ as the head of the subject noun phrase limits what can be in the noun phrase with it. _Those_ could have been _the, these, some_, but not much else. There could have been an adjective between that word and the noun _boys_ such as: _those young/little/big boys_. That's a larger group of choices but it is still limited to features of _boys_. _Were_ is limited to a plural past form of _be_, and so on. The sentence pattern itself limits the choices the writer and the reader have. In English, word order is usually quite limiting. Subject typically precedes the verb and the object typically follows it. Adjectives such as _good_ precede the noun they modify. _Some_ expresses an indefinite amount.

Redundancy is obvious in the examples above. But it is even more pervasive if we consider that at each level of language, the choices we make at one place reduce the possibilities of what can follow or pattern with them.

Certain sounds can follow other sounds and others can not. For example, in English we can end a sentence with a sequence of /g/ followed immediately by /d/ as in the words *bagged* or *sagged*, but we can't start a word that way (as one can in Polish—Gdansk is the name of a Polish city).

In English spelling the letter <q> will almost always require <u> to follow. Computer word processors can suggest a few likely letter sequences, words, or phrases that can follow as you start to type based on limitations of what is likely to follow. A GPS can be programmed to limit the possible next letters as you enter a city or street in entering the address you want directions to.

I've used the term *limiting* here to indicate that the readers know a lot about what can follow, precede, or pattern with any word or phrase, but that does not mean that they can predict the specific words that will appear. In that sense there is a great deal of redundancy. In the next chapter on wording, Peter shows the potential number of meanings any word sequence could have. In reality, the reader is seldom aware of the multiple meanings because of the redundancy that limits choices. The way a grammatical pattern begins signals the reader what can possibly follow that constrains what the reader can predict. Predicting a pattern such as S V IO DO provides information of what is likely to follow (for example, He gave her the book). And the meaning already understood gives advance information of what follows.

So language is both ambiguous and redundant. And with our set for ambiguity and our ability to use the redundancy to predict and infer where the text is going, making sense of a text can be quite efficient—much more efficient than sequentially recognizing words. We have so much redundant information that our eyes need to fixate on only about two thirds of the words and we still make sense of it; we can sample selectively enough from the text using only the most useful and necessary cues to construct our meaning.

Hebrew and Arabic work quite well, even though they are normally written without most of the vowels. In one study, the researcher presented a single written sentence to adult readers of Arabic and asked them to think of as many readings that sentence could have if the vowel subscripts had all been provided. Without context, the readers were likely to think of one or two of the most likely ones whereas there were nine or more different possibilities. The subjects told him that when they read they use the context to know what the words are without the vowels. Without the vowels, the texts are quite ambiguous, but in context there is so much redundancy that Arabic and Hebrew readers have little trouble reading even though the vowels aren't represented (Al Fahid and Goodman, 2008).

Here's an important fact: No writing is complete. There are aspects of the system of language missing. Alphabetic writing does a poor job of representing emotion. About the best it offers is the exclamation point, bold face, and font. But the reader has to supply the tone and feeling not represented in the text. Chinese phonology uses tone to differentiate meanings—Cantonese has nine tones, for example. So the same character may mean different things depending on the tone of oral Chinese but tone is not marked so the reader must assign it in order to make sense of the text. The meaning of an English sentence changes—even its grammar—depending on which word gets stressed but that's not usually marked either.

Any statement can become a question just by changing the intonation patterns.

> Poor Freddie was in trouble again.
> Poor Freddie was in trouble again?

The lesson in all this is that the system works despite its faults—and if it were more complete it would be too hard to use. In any case, the success of any language act depends on the language user. The reader must infer what is missing in the written text.

# References

Al Fahid, J. M. and Goodman, K. S. (2008). "The reading process in Arabic: Making sense of Arabic print." In Flurkey, A. D., Paulson, E. J. and Goodman, K. S. (Eds.), *Scientific realism in studies of reading* (pp. 155–168). New York: Lawrence Erlbaum Associates.

Dahl, R. (1953). *Someone like you.* New York: Knopf.

Dahl, R. (1958). "Poison." In Inglis, R. B. and Spear, J. (Eds.), *Adventures in English literature* (pp. 604–611). New York: Harcourt, Brace.

Dewey, J. and Bentley, A. F. (1949). *Knowing and the known.* Boston, MA: Beacon Press.

Halliday, M. A. K. (2004a). "Three aspects of children's language development: Learning language, learning through language, learning about language." In Webster, J. (Ed.), *The language of early childhood. Volume 4 in the collected works of M.A.K. Halliday* (pp. 308–326). New York: Continuum.

Halliday, M. A. K. (2004b). "Towards a language-based theory of learning." In Webster, J. (Ed.), *The language of early childhood. Volume 4 in the collected works of M.A.K. Halliday,* (pp. 327–352). New York: Continuum.

Moore, L. (1965). "Freddie Miller, Scientist." In Betts, E. and Welch, C. (Eds.), *Adventures here and there* (pp. 61–68). New York: American Book Company.

Rosenblatt, L. M. (1978). *The reader, the text, the poem: The transactional theory of the literary work.* Carbondale: Southern Illinois University.

# Words on Words and Wording  **6**

Polonius: What do you read, my lord?
Hamlet: Words, words, words.

 In this chapter, we compare two views of words in language and particularly in reading. The first view, which has dominated reading instruction, is that the major goal in reading is learning words and learning how to identify them. Terms such as *word attack*, *word recognition*, and *sight words* are often used by advocates of this word-oriented approach to describe what readers must do to be successful readers.

In the last chapter, we presented our view of how texts convey meaning. We discussed wording as a process in which grammar and word choice are made at the same time since the form that words take and the company they keep among other words depends on each other. Grammatical patterns limit word choice and word choice limits grammatical patterns. But there has been so much focus on words in the research on reading that we need to examine carefully in this chapter just what words are and what they aren't and why reading cannot be considered simply word identification.

For an example of how these two views influence instruction, here is how one reader read this sentence from *Mrs. Frisbee and the Rats of NIHM* (O'Brien and Bernstein, 1971):

**Table 6.1** Miscue Example

<table>
<tr><td>*I   understand*<br>Now he understood why the children</td></tr>
<tr><td>*have                my*<br>had been calling his name.</td></tr>
</table>

In this reading, the reader changes an indirect quote to a direct quote. That has the result of changing the whole sentence to present tense from past tense and from third person to first person. So *understood* is switched to *understand* and *had* is changed to *have*. That shows the reader treating these as alternate forms of the same word. *He* also has shifted to *I* and *his* to *my*. And, of course, the meaning of the whole is really unchanged. This is a beautiful example of how wording involves word choice and grammar at the same time. But in a word recognition view, the reader has read four wrong words.

To make the case against the illusion that reading is essentially word identification, we'll be using examples such as this from our large database of readers reading real texts and from the huge word banks Peter, as a linguist, can access on his computer. We'll provide evidence that recognizing words is a lot more complicated than it seems.

## The Wording of Texts: What Counts as a Word?

### The Nature of Words

Certainly the notion of word is among the most prominent of language concepts. The Bible says, "In the beginning was the word." When parents talk of their toddlers, they focus on, "How many words does she know?" Many people think of learning a foreign language as consisting primarily of learning the words (the vocabulary) of that language.

In writing alphabetic language, we separate words with spaces. But actually, word space came to alphabetic writing quite late. Early writing systems did not mark word boundaries, and even today in Chinese and Japanese all characters are equally spaced with no markings for word boundaries. Indeed there is considerable discussion among Chinese linguists as to whether the concept of word is useful in the description of Chinese.

The written English word, while it seems easy to see and identify, is nonetheless a complicated concept.

## What's a Word? Word Forms

Let's go back to the beginning of *Freddie Miller, Scientist* (Moore, 1965), which served us well in the last chapter:

> Poor Freddie was in trouble again. He had been experimenting with his chemistry set, and Elizabeth's doll had turned green.
>
> His little sister was heartbroken. Freddie's mother was angry.
>
> "You've wrecked that doll!" she exclaimed. "What queer experiment was it this time?"
>
> "I was only washing the doll to make it look like new," Freddie explained. "I made a special mixture. But I guess I added too many chemicals to the mixture."
>
> "I guess you did," Mrs. Miller said. "You are just like your Uncle August—never letting well enough alone."
>
> Freddie had heard a lot about Uncle August, and a lot about his other uncles, too. All of them were living in Switzerland, where Mrs. Miller had grown up. She was always comparing Freddie with them.
>
> Good or bad, he was always like one of the uncles!

My laptop computer can count the words in this short section or a database of several million words in a few seconds. The word-count program on my computer says that this passage has 139 words. Yes it does, but only if you count every word of the passage. But *uncle* appears two times though once it is *Uncle* and once it is *uncle*. And the word *uncles* is also there twice. Should we regard these as four different words, or four instances of the same word? If we wish to count words in running text, we have to count those occurrences as four words. However, if we wish to measure the variety of vocabulary used in this text we need to treat them as four instances of the same word.

If we disregard differences between capital and lower case letters, this passage uses 82 word types. Of these 82 word types, 25 (30 percent) of these word types occur more than once—that is, they have more than one token. In most longer texts (over 2000 words), roughly half of the word types are used only once. One reason this portion of a text contains so few repeated words is that the text is so short. Typically, function words are most common in any text. In this one, *was* (seven tokens) and *I* (five tokens) are the most frequent. In longer English texts, *the* and *of* are usually the most frequent words.

Grouping *uncle* and *uncles* into a single category results in what linguists call a *lemma*. The lemma UNCLE contains two types—two word forms. This passage contains another group of word types (*are, been, was, were*). As differently as they are spelled, they still belong to the same lemma BE.

In our miscue research, our subjects seemed to treat them as forms of a lemma that are interchangeable depending on context. For this discussion, to be clear, we'll use a few more linguistic conventions. *Uncles* is composed of two morphemes: {uncle} and {-s}. Morphemes are the smallest units of language that can convey meaning. In this case {uncle} is the base, and the {-s} is a bound morpheme attached to the base. In English, in addition to the plural {-s} there is the possessive {-s} (as in Freddie's mother) and the third-person singular present tense form (as in the final /s/ on *walk* in *he walks*).

Some bound morphemes are inflectional. Noun inflections include the plural and possessive affixes; verb inflections include the third-person present tense (*experiments*), the past tense (*experimented*—without a helping verb) the past participle *experimented* (as in *had experimented*) and the present participle *experimenting* (as in *was experimenting*); some adjectives and adverbs accept the inflectional morphemes {-er} (*longer*) and {-est} (*longest*).

By contrast, derivational bound morphemes create new words. Examples include suffixes such as {-ture} in words such as *mixture* and *texture*, {-al} as in *arrival* and *denial*, the suffix {-en} as in *brighten* and *heart-broken*, the prefix {en-} as in *enlarge* and *endear*, and {infra-} as in *infrared, infrasonic,* and *infrastructure.*

Though we are trying to avoid using too much jargon in this book, we need enough terminology to keep the concepts straight. So let's recap:

**types** (word types): distinct words.
**tokens** (word tokens): the actual appearances of each word type in a text.
**morpheme**: a word or word part that is the smallest language unit that has meaning potential.
**free morpheme**: a morpheme that can occur in a text as a complete word or as part of a word with affixes attached to it.

**bound morpheme**: a morpheme that never occurs as a complete word. In English, most bound morphemes are affixes attached to a free morpheme.
**lemma**: all the various forms a morpheme and its affixes can take.
**orthographic words**: all words that have identical spellings. This includes:

- words that have several uses and meanings, such as the main verb *have* and the helping verb *have*.
- instances of different words that are spelled the same way such as *bank* (the financial institution and the edge of a river), or *sink* (the place where you wash dishes and the verb).
- the various forms of lemmas such as the verb BE (*am, are, is, was, were, being, been,* and *be*) would all be treated as separate orthographic words.

When your computer tells you how many words you have written, it simply counts orthographic words. Needless to say, it is dangerous to rely on word counts that merely count orthographic words, because you don't know the significance of what is being counted.

 Basal readers control vocabulary using new words as often as possible disregarding differences in grammatical function or meaning. But our readers' miscues reflected confusion in attempting to make sense of these texts.

In one story from a second grade basal, the word *circus* had a few miscues as a noun—fo example, *He went to the circus.* But more miscues occurred when it was used as a noun modifier—for example, *He met a circus man.*

## WORD MEANINGS

Of course the concept of word is useful because it is associated with meanings. We are not interested in the lemma REMAIN merely because the word forms *remain, remains, remaining,* and *remained* all have related **forms**. These words express **meanings** that are related in predictable ways. We also can relate these forms to some other words such as *remainder* and *remnant*.

And we must distinguish word forms that have the same appearance but different meanings. All languages have words that look or sound alike but have very different meanings. For example, the word form *pool* appears in sentences such as:

He went to the pool to swim.
We decided to pool our resources.

Dictionaries show them as two different words with different definitions. Words also have varied meanings in varied contexts. The most common words typically have the most different meanings. The OED mentions over 37 different numbered (= major) meanings for *set* used as a noun, and more than 50 for *set* used as a verb. (This count ignores meanings listed as obsolete or technical.) Even less common words such as *count* have several meanings. For example:

> Johnny can *count* to five.
> We spent our time *counting* the sheets.
> His opinion doesn't *count*.
> We have a staff of ten if you *count* the part time folks.
> We are *counting* on him for the picnic supplies.
> At 62, his age could *count* against him.
> *Count* Radziwill is the local nobleman.

## FROZEN COMBINATIONS OF WORDS THAT ARE USED AS SINGLE UNITS

The focus on words as sequences of letters surrounded by space gets us into another problem. Some word sequences have special meanings as a whole. The *idiom "Slip through the cracks"* has nothing to do with slipping or cracks. Most people believe that idioms are uncommon. However, if we change the definition slightly to include sequences of words that are treated as a single meaning unit, we will find that much of the English used in both writing and speaking, particularly in casual conversation, consists of such sequences.

*I guess you did* and *leaving well enough alone* in the passage from *Freddie Miller* (Moore, 1965) are both examples of phrases that aren't idioms but have unique meanings as common phrases.

When I looked at the word *view* in a corpus of slightly less than six million words of text, I found 1226 occurrences as a noun, 213 tokens (17 percent) were in the phrase *point of view*, and another 84 tokens (6.6 percent) were in *in view of. On view* occurred but much less frequently. Notice that in each case the interpretation of the whole phrase is related to the usual meaning of *view* but the phrase is used to mean something special.

Children and second language learners often show that these are meaning units when they misuse them. One three year old said, "Wait a few whiles." After reading a story, a Samoan fourth grader answered the question, "How did he feel?" with "He felt with his leg."

## The Wording of a Particular Text

In 1976 to celebrate the 200th anniversary of the Declaration of Independence, the journal *Visible Language* published a "Declaration of Independence Kit" (Perrin, 1976). It consisted of all the letters and punctuation marks in the Declaration arranged in alphabetic order, so many a's, b's, etc. Obviously, an alphabetic text is a collection of letters but a text is certainly more than that. And if we made a similar alphabetic list of all the words in the Declaration, it would be a lot more than that, too.

One way to look at how words pattern in actual language is what Peter and other corpus linguists are doing with very large databases of coherent language. Those databases consist of many texts carefully chosen to represent some portion of the English language used at the time they were gathered. But another way to see how words pattern in actual language is to closely examine the wording of individual texts (see Table 6.2). This is the approach Lois Bird (now known as Lois Bridges) and I used with six texts that had been used in our multi-population miscue studies (Goodman and Bird, 1984). *Freddie Miller* (Moore, 1965) was one of those texts. Our concern in this study was to see how the wording of the text is constrained by the nature of the text.

The six texts ranged from fourth grade level to an adult opinion piece, "Generation Gap" (Rapoport, 1970).

**Table 6.2** Representations of Grammatical Categories

| | Percent of Running Words | | | | | |
|---|---|---|---|---|---|---|
| | Freddie | Genius | Ghost | Sheep Dog | Poison | Gap |
| Pronouns* | 9.3 | 11.6 | 4.9 | 6.7 | 11.8 | 6.9 |
| Other Nouns | 21.5 | 17.9 | 24.5 | 22.8 | 16.1 | 20.6 |
| Other Noun Positions | 30.8 | 29.5 | 29.4 | 29.5 | 27.9 | 27.5 |
| Verbs | 17.6 | 18.3 | 15.3 | 15.4 | 18.4 | 17.5 |
| Noun Modifiers* | 10.2 | 10.7 | 10.7 | 10.2 | 8.8 | 11.6 |
| Verb Modifiers | 4.6 | 4 | 4.8 | 4.1 | 5.8 | 3.1 |
| Function Words | 32.7 | 32.1 | 37.6 | 38.7 | 36.4 | 38.9 |
| Indeterminate | 0 | 7 | 0.2 | 0.1 | 0.3 | 0 |
| Contractions | 2.3 | 4.2 | 0.6 | 0.6 | 2.2 | 0.6 |

* Possessive pronouns are included as noun modifiers

## Proportions of Grammatical Functions

All the texts we looked at had about the same proportions of nouns, verbs, adjectives, adverbs, and function words. The only category that shows much variation from text to text is the proportion of pronouns varying from 4.9 percent to almost 12 percent. What is important is that about a third of the words in any of these texts are function words which set up the grammatical context for the text to make sense.

Much of these proportions of grammatical categories and function-word frequency are the direct result of how syntax works in English. Noun phrases usually require determiners (mostly *the* or *a*) in English and a sentence could have several noun phrases but usually only one verb per clause.

In considering word frequency, frequency in the language as a whole and the frequency of the word or phrase in each individual text are quite different measures. The general social interaction in which a text appears also affects the wording choices. (Wording always involves choices in both words **and** grammar.) People tend to choose similar language (words and grammar) when they engage in similar sorts of interactions. The language used in a socially recognized type of interaction is called a register.

Of the six texts reported in Table 6.2, four are stories written for children, one is a popular story written for adults, and one is an opinion piece intended for a popular audience. They represent similar genres.

But consider the relative use of nouns and verbs in individual texts. Nouns and verbs are not simply words; nouns do different sorts of grammatical tasks in sentences than verbs do. In Table 6.2, the total noun positions hovers around 30 percent for all. The verbs range from 15.3 percent to 18.4 percent of the vocabulary of each story. The only variable is the relative proportion of pronouns, with a range of 4.9–11.8.

However, it is important to see how noun phrases, prepositional phrases, and verb phrases are used in the texts. What proportion of each text is found within a noun phrase, prepositional phrase, or verb phrase? How many clauses describe actions (*He ran to the cellar*) and how many simply describe some entity? (*His little sister was heartbroken*).

There is also what I call the Rule of Economy in Language: once something is known it does not need to be repeated. The first reference to a tree may be *The big old oak tree*. After that, it is *the tree* or even *it*. So adjectives are often not repeated after their first use. Similarly, adverbs don't need to be repeated.

The most common word in all six stories was *the*. That one word occurred 370 times in *Sheep Dog* (Stovall, 1966). That is almost 10 percent of all running words. In *Generation Gap* (Rapoport, 1970) there were 269 *the*'s and it was also close to one-tenth of all running words. The first five most common words in each text ranged from 15–20 percent of the total running words in each story. And the most common 25 different words in each story were about 40 percent of all the words in each story. Yet only eight words appear on all six lists. All are function words except *it* which is a pronoun. They are (with their mean rank): the (1) and (4.5) to (4.5) a (6.3) of (8.3) in (10.8) it (12.8) that (15.5).

*Sheep Dog* (Stovall, 1966) centers on a dog protecting a band of sheep from coyotes so there is very little dialog. Similarly *Ghost of the Lagoon* (Sperry, 1967) is about a boy and his dog on an island, and the shark who dominates the lagoon, again with little dialog. In *My Brother is a Genius* (Hayes, 1963), *said* occurs 51 times because the boy and the baby say words from the dictionary. The grammar of dialog requires an extra clause we call dialog carriers with the form: (someone) said "some expression."

Contractions are also more common in texts with a lot of dialog. While we are on the subject of dialog, our miscue research showed a somewhat surprising phenomenon. While sections of texts that contain dialog are relatively complex grammatically, they are not likely to involve high proportions of miscues for readers. Writers use dialog to give the readers a sense of listening in on the conversations of the characters.

In each of the six texts, more than half of all different words (types)

 Consider a very different text—an abstract for an article in a medical journal which belongs to a different register with a very different intended audience. Since it introduces a case report of the treatments of two individuals it includes some narration; not all narratives belong to the same register.

In the 2920 word abstract, 62 percent of the words are in noun phrases with a major function (such as subject or object, etc.) in the clauses. The combination of nouns, pronouns, and noun modifiers in the six texts Ken discusses was about 40 percent. There were only 10 (3 percent) pronouns, eight of them appearing in the narrative portions of the abstract. There were only eight determiners (*the*, *a*, or *this*), of which six appear in the narrative portion. I found 44 (15 percent) verbs that functioned either as (part of) a main verb in a main or subordinate clause.

The noun phrases in the abstract regularly differ in their internal structures and their functions in the sentences of the various texts in Table 6.2. So the register to which a text belongs also strongly affects the frequencies with which various vocabulary and grammatical choices are made.

occurred only once. In *Generation Gap* (Rapoport, 1970), three-fourths of all types occurred only once. That shows a stylistic difference from the narratives in the other five texts. On the other hand, half of all the running words in all six texts are represented by as few as 7 percent of the different types.

The bulk of the words in every text are function words which create the grammatical frames for the less frequent words that have meaning potential. While the majority of the 25 most common word types are function words and pronouns, there is still room for stylistic variety.

## Uncommon Words Are Common

What stands out when we look at most common content words in each story is that the only nouns that are common at all are proper nouns—usually the names of the characters. In fact we can say that words common in a given text may be quite uncommon in Peter's databases. There are two reasons for this: one, of course, is the focus or plot of the text; the other is a strong tendency in English to avoid repeating the same nouns, verbs, adjectives, and adverbs. So the author chooses synonyms or other devices to avoid repetitious use of words.

There are 11 references to the *canoe* in *Ghost of the Lagoon* (Sperry, 1967) but only two use the word *canoe*. In the opening sequence of Roald Dahl's *Poison* (1958), the main character arrives home and goes in the house. Eleven different verb phrases are used to represent the movement into the house. So there are several strong cohesive chains in each story.

Can you tell from the most common words listed below what each story was about?

| | |
|---|---|
| *Freddie*: | Uncle, mother, father, said |
| *Genius*: | baby, typical |
| *Ghost*: | canoe, water |
| *Sheep Dog*: | sheep, coyote(s), band |
| *Poison*: | said, now |
| *Gap*: | children |

*Said* is the only verb in any Top 25 list. Only one adjective or adverb is common enough to make any of the lists.

Let's sum up: the wording of any text uses a matrix of function words which, though they carry little definable meaning, make it possible to create a text in which some content words will be used more frequently than others and most words will occur only once. But there's more to what makes a text comprehensible than that.

## The Role of Grammar in Wording the Text

The middle level of our cuing systems or Halliday's strata is the level of *lexicogrammar*—the level of where grammatical and word choices are made at the same time (Halliday, 2004). As we read, we have to use grammatical information, assigning a structure as we leap toward making sense. The words can only represent meaning in some sentence (syntactic) structure. I've created some stories in which I replaced all the content words with non-words. The non-words seem to take on meaning because of how the structures frame them. Here's a favorite (Goodman, 1996): A Mardsan Giberter for Farfie

> Glis was very fraper. She had denarpen Farfie's mardsan. She didn't talp a giberter for him.
> So she conlanted to plimp a mardsan binky for him. She had just sparved the binky when he jibbled in the gorger.
> "Clorsty mardsan!," she boffed.
> "That's a crouistish mardsan binky," boffed Farfie, "but my mardsan is on Stansan. Agsan is Kelsan."
> "In that ruspen," boffed Glis, "I won't whank you your giberter til Stansan."

In Table 6.3, I've left the function words unchanged since they frame the grammar of this story. But you know the grammatical function of each nonsense word. The subject of the first sentence is *Glis*, of course. And *Glis* is probably a name, a proper noun. How do you know that? If it were not a proper noun, there would have been an article, *a* or *the*, before it. And the next paragraph confirms this because a pronoun, *she*, replaces the subject. So *Glis* is feminine. *Fraper* is an adjective. We know that because the verb is a form of be (*was*) and *very* comes before *fraper*. So this pattern is a common one: the adjective modifies the subject. The next sentence has the verb *denarpen*. We know it's a verb for several reasons:

- It follows *had* and has an -en ending.
- It's between the subject—*she*—and the object—*Farfie's mardsan*.
- Furthermore, you can predict the other forms this verb would have: *denarp*, *denarps*, *denarping*, *denarped*.

*Farfie* is another character in this story. He is male we know from the pronouns.

You can see three cues to the structure of English at work in this story (see Table 6.3).

**Table 6.3** A Mardsan Giberter for Farfie

1. **Sequence:** The sequence of the parts of each clause is important in English grammar. SVO (subject + verb + object) is very common.

2. **Inflection:** Word endings are used to show functions of nouns and verbs. The -en, and -ed endings here are examples. Nouns in English don't have many case endings. In this story we have the possessive, *Farfie's*.

3. The function words set up the patterns for the content words.

```
A Mardsan Giberter for Farfie
---- was very -----. She had -----en
-----'s ------. She didn't ---- a ------
for him.
So she -------ed to ----- a ------ -----
for
him. She had just ----ed the -----
when
he -----ed in the -----.

"----- ------- !", she -----ed.
"That's a -------- ------- -----," ----ed -
----,
"but my ------ is on ------. ----- is ------
."
In that -----", ----ed ----, "I won't ----
you
      your ------ til --------.
```

When I write a nonsense story like this, I have to start with a real story. That may explain why when I use this story with a large group there are always a few people who can reconstruct the original story from these bare bones. Can you figure it out?

A fourth signal also cues/signals what an utterance (linguists prefer this term to sentence as a meaningful unit of oral language) means. As we said above, we can tell what grammatical structure a reader has chosen from the intonation in oral reading.

Any statement can be turned into a question by changing the intonation:

That boy was elected president of his class. (Falling intonation)
That boy was elected president of his class? (Rising intonation)

Then we can change the meaning of the sentence by changing the word that we stress in it:

**That** boy was elected president of his class? The one over there? Not a
    different boy?

That **boy** was elected president of his class. Not a girl? Not a man?

That boy was **elected** president of his class. Elected not appointed?

That boy was elected **president** of his class. Not secretary?

That boy was elected president of his **class**. Not his school?

English has many pairs of words such as *record/record, desert/desert,
produce/produce, import/import, present/present*, etc. In these pairs, the words
that stress the first syllable are nouns while the words that stress the second
syllable are verbs.

What is important to understand is that intonation signals various grammatical relations and does much more than express emotions. Intonation used
over sentences or sentence parts makes it possible for oral language to use
much more complex relations among the parts of the sentences, and so
sentences in typical spoken language (where there are no interruptions) tend
to be longer and more complex than sentences in the written language.

## Interdependence of Grammar and Word Choice in Wording of Texts

There is a long tradition in discussions of language that
separates grammar from vocabulary. In this view, the
grammatical structure provides a framework within which
speakers (writers) place the vocabulary they wish to use, and
the choice of grammatical structure and the choice of
vocabulary do not influence one another.

But studies of very large collections of texts with 300 to 500 million words
of running text find a close relation between the choice of vocabulary and the
sorts of grammatical constructions used. The speaker or writer chooses the
meaning and the means to express those meanings at the same time. Each
limits the other. The listener or reader must also assign a grammatical structure
to make sense of the wording of a text.

### Making Sense of a Multitude of Meanings

Words, grammar, and meanings are all closely related. Words take specific
meaning only in particular grammatical relationships with the other words in

**Table 6.4** Word Meanings In A Sentence From A Fourth Grader

| Word meanings in a sentence from a fourth grade reader | | | | | | | | | |
|---|---|---|---|---|---|---|---|---|---|
| After | the | cut | in | his | allowance, | Freddie's | chemistry | experiments | narrowed |
| 22 | 19 | 26 | 56 | 2 | 4 | 1 | 3 | 3 | 6 |
| to | | those | safely | outlined | | in | a | library | book. |
| 20 | | 4 | 2 | 3 | | 56 | 11 | 2 | 9 |

the context. Treating words as items to be identified and interpreted as separate entities is not simply a theoretical mistake, it leads to serious complications for readers in comprehending. For example, what would a reader have to do to read and understand the following sentence from Freddie *(FM)*.

> After the cut in his allowance, Freddie's chemistry experiments narrowed to those safely outlined in a library book.

If we are first to identify each word, and then relate it to its context, we not only have to recognize a sequence of letters, we also need to identify the range of meanings that that word potentially represents.

Of course, locating all the meanings that are potentially expressed by a particular word gets very complex. Table 6.4 provides each word of the sentence and below it the number of meanings listed in a simple desk dictionary for each of them.

The box below indicates that *after* has 22 meanings and *the* has 19 meanings. In order to determine how many combinations of the meanings of those two words result, one multiplies 22 times 19 (that results in 418 possible combinations). In order to calculate how many combinations of word meanings are possible in the entire sentence, we merely continue to multiply every number by every other number. The result is 399, 316, 187, 709, 440. Not all combinations would make sense. But how can the reader consider which of the many possible combinations could make sense?

This calculation indicates only the number of potential combinations of **word** meanings. The sentence contains at least two grammatical constructions that themselves introduce multiple interpretations. It contains two instances of a possessive with a noun construction (*his allowance* and *Freddie's chemistry experiments*) and two instances of a noun + noun sequence (*chemistry* *experiments* and *library book*). Each of these constructions allows several interpretations.

The phrase *his allowance* can be interpreted in at least the following ways:

- Is it the allowance made for him?
- Or the allowance he made for someone or something else?
- Is the allowance a thing like *he got a weekly allowance?*
- Or a more abstract thing like *we make allowances for him?*
- And how can an allowance be cut? With a knife?

Similarly, there are several meanings possible when a noun is used as a noun modifier as in *chemistry experiments*.

- Are the experiments in a chemistry class?
- Are they composed of chemistry?
- Are they experiments that involve the use of chemistry? Or chemicals (a different word)?

- And are the experiments trying out chemistry or more formal experiments a scientist might conduct?
- And in what sense can someone possess chemistry experiments (his)?
- And ultimately how can chemistry experiments be outlined safely (or otherwise) in a library book?

Each possibility adds to the number of possible interpretations of this seemingly simple statement. In order to continue to calculate the mathematically possible combinations of meanings in this sentence, we need to discover how many *different interpretations* are possible.

## Efficiency in Wording

Clearly, if readers had to check each potential combination of meanings for each sentence as they read, even ordinary sentences such as this one would take days or months to process, not a fraction of a second. Of course, only a small fraction of the meaning combinations arrived at in this way make any sense at all. And of those, only a very small group will be found to be appropriate to the meaning of the text at that point. Of course, the point behind the discussion above is that only if readers must identify each successive word is this huge variation possible. Efficient readers do not have to process anything like that number of meanings.

Efficient readers make sense of the text. They use cues from the text to assign a grammatical structure and to anticipate what will follow. They do not need to choose from the multiple meanings of each word or word combination because as they build meaning only limited choices are possible. They chunk the words that have frozen meanings as they work at making sense. They are processing word sequences, phrases, and other larger constructions of language as they construct relevant meanings from what they perceive. The central thesis of this book is that reading is an efficient process of making sense of written language. It would be quite impossible for readers to first recognize words and then make sense of the whole. Steve has described forward loops in the brain. Each decision we make in constructing meaning carries with it a prediction of what can follow. That makes subsequent text redundant; we already know roughly what's coming so we only need to sample it to confirm/check our predictions.

## How Text Complexity Is Reflected in Miscues

To consider how text complexity is reflected in readers' miscues, Susanne Gespass and I used data from miscue studies (Goodman and Gespass, 1983). We used a formula developed by Australian Des Ryan (1978) to rate the miscues

**Table 6.5** Sentence Score for Sentence 22

| Sentence SCORE 2.76 |
| --- |
| 2.30   1.86   1.39    6.51    5.24   8.60 |
| After the cut in his allowance, Freddie's chemistry |
| 5.88        4.52   .5   .71   4.98    2.93 |
| experiments narrowed to those safely outlined |
| .18   1.89    1.37    .17 |
| in   a    library    book |

that occurred on each element in each sentence including the one we are discussing. In this system, if the ratings of the miscues on a word are higher, the miscues are of lower quality and/or there are more miscues on that word. That gave us a rating of text complexity for the sentence and for each word in it.

This sentence 22 (see Table 6.5) was the fifth most complex in the story, *Freddie Miller* (Moore, 1965).

Here is its ratings. Notice that seven of the eighteen words have a score higher than the score for the sentence as a whole. *The* and *in* in the first line had no score because there were no miscues on those words.

Of course, the vocabulary choices made in a text may themselves pose difficulties for readers and so contribute to higher miscue scores. For example, the words *allowance, chemistry, experiments,* and *narrowed* are often difficult for young readers and that word-based difficulty contributes to the high scores for those words.

## Synactic Complexity

But vocabulary difficulty is not the only reason readers may miscue while reading a sentence. Reader miscues also often reflect syntactic complexity. Even when readers encounter words that are familiar to them—but appear in unfamiliar surroundings—the miscue scores are likely to increase.

Let's examine this complexity through the miscues on this sentence. Below we unpack the sentence into clauses intended to represent the meaning and underlying assumptions more explicitly. The original sentence has been divided into three major parts and is presented in italics.

*After the cut in his allowance*
After (his mother) cut the (money) allowance that she (?) (usually) gave
 him,
*Freddie's chemistry experiments narrowed to*
Freddie had to restrict his experiments to
*Those safely outlined in a library book*
Those that had been outlined (meaning in this case laid out) in a library
 book and were assumed to be safe.

It is instructive to see how much information is packed into the initial prepositional phrase *after the cut in his allowance*. Although the word *cut* is a noun in this phrase, it actually describes an action. But the two major participants in the action: the actor (the person who did the cutting), and the thing that got cut are not expressed in this phrase. Normally this sort of prepositional phrase (one that includes a noun that describes an action) is used to summarize some action that has been previously described and relates that action to the action in the main clause of the sentence. This is the case for *after the cut in Freddie's allowance*. This phrase refers back to an earlier line in which Freddie's mother says, *"I want you to save half your allowance for it* [= buying a new doll for Elizabeth] *each week."* So sensitive readers who see the relation between that sentence and the phrase *after the cut in his allowance* know who did the cutting and what was cut.

But a comparison of the wordings of the earlier sentence with the phrase *after the cut in his allowance* reveals very little similarity between the two. Only one word appears in both and that is *allowance*. In fact, the connection requires considerable inferencing to interpret.

- Readers must interpret Freddie's mother saying *I want you to save half your allowance* as a command—you **will** save. . . .
- The word *allowance* must be interpreted as a sum of money that is regularly given to Freddie (*allowance* appears later in the story with quite a different meaning).
- Saving half the allowance to buy a doll for Elizabeth must be seen as reducing the allowance available to Freddie to choose what to spend it on (and hence it constitutes cutting the allowance).

In short, it takes a great deal of linguistic, cultural, and inferential knowledge for a reader to interpret the earlier sentence as describing Freddie's mother cutting his allowance.

*Allowance* may also be a somewhat unfamiliar word to these readers. It occurs earlier with the same meaning and has a similar score. It also occurs later in a different grammatical context and meaning (*We must make some allowance* . . .) and has a much lower address score of 3.66 in that context. So in sentence 22 the high-syntactic complexity must be contributing to the high miscue scores on this word.

In the main clause, the verb *narrowed to* is a metaphor—the range of chemistry experiments was limited, either by Freddie or by Freddie's mother—we are not told which. Then comes the third phrase that needs unpacking: *those safely outlined in a library book. Safely outlined* is complex because it is not the outlining which is safe but the experiments which are safe. The adjective *safe* has been changed to adverb *safely* and applied to the verb. Here is another grammatical metaphor.

The final prepositional phrase *in a library book* requires the reader to infer:

- that experiments may be outlined in a book (of course, readers who know what outlined means may wonder why that verb was chosen rather than *described*);
- that such a book can be obtained from a library (potentially);
- that someone has made finding the experiment in a library book a condition of any further experimenting for Freddie; and
- that being described or outlined in a library book implies that the experiment will be safe.

Among 32 readers, 12 substituted *the* for *a* in the phrase *a library book*. Three readers corrected their miscue. Some readers apparently couldn't handle all of the needed inferences. They anticipated *the library* rather than *a library book*. We know that because *library* would take the definite *the* while library book would be indefinite with *a*. This is evidence that the reader is assigning a grammatical and a meaning structure in making sense of this complicated sentence. (Of course, readers could have thought that the experiments were outlined in a specific book. Certainly that is a potential reading if we feel that Freddie was required to find the experiments in a particular book.)

The patterns of miscues associated with this sentence help us to understand how the two aspects of wording combine to influence the reading. *Safely* is not an uncommon word but the miscue score on that word is much higher than *outlined*. That probably is the result of the readers coping with the sense in which *outlining* can be safe or unsafe.

The word *the* typically occasions few miscues in any text, but the miscues in which readers say *they cut* or *he cut* instead of *the cut* suggest that these readers have not figured out that Freddie's mother is the one responsible for cutting Freddie's allowance.

Similarly, nine of our readers said *the allowance* for *his allowance*. This miscue retains the definiteness of the noun phrase, but loses the meaning that it is Freddie's allowance. The text required the readers to infer more than some of them were able to do.

*Freddie's chemistry experiments* begins with the possessive form, *Freddie's*. Many readers, expecting the subject noun to be the first word in the phrase, substitute *Freddy* for *Freddie's* and then expect *chemistry* to be a verb.

Given the potentially misleading local grammatical contexts in which *Freddie's, chemistry, experiments,* and *narrowed* appear, it is not surprising that these words all have high scores.

I've discussed this single sentence in depth to show that comprehension is much more than identifying the words the writer has chosen but also is affected by the way they come together and the grammatical context in which they occur. Familiar words may be involved in miscues in unfamiliar uses and unfamiliar words may be understood within the particular contexts they occur in a text.

## Grammar and Meaning

In all this meaning construction, the reader is using both grammar and meaning. A tentative grammatical pattern is assigned and the reader constructs meaning using cues from that pattern and the words, word patterns, and word parts.

Since writers are choosing vocabulary and grammar at the same time, there are strong tendencies for words to occur:

• in certain grammatical constructions and not in others; and
• in the company of certain words, but not in others.

From their experience with language use, readers and listeners have intuitive knowledge of which are the most likely meanings for these combinations. Similarly when we look at grammatical patterns such as N + V + N (*I got a book*), or N + V + N + N (*I got him a book*), we find that certain patterns regularly contain certain words and not others. Finally, all these patterns of occurrence and non-occurrence correlate (in complicated ways) with the meanings expressed.

## So What Makes a Text Comprehensible?

Let's sum up: the wording of any text uses a matrix of function words which, though they carry little definable meaning, make it possible to create a text in which some content words will be used more frequently than others and most words will occur only once. But there's more to what makes a text comprehensible than that.

In this chapter we've shown that language is a lot more than a collection of words. The wording of any text is closely connected with the choice of language structure; grammar depends on word choice and word choice depends on grammar. Of course words take various forms depending on where they fit in a pattern so it is natural for a writer or reader to use the appropriate form for a verb (past, present, etc.), for nouns (singular, plural, etc.), and so forth. The particular wording of a story or other type of text depends on what it is about. So words uncommon in the language can be common in a single text.

But we also considered that in every language there are words that look or sound alike that are very different words with very different meanings. We hope we've made the point that a word has no meaning except in the company of other words. But in grammatical context and with other words close by, meaning becomes unambiguous and the reader will seldom be aware that there were other possible meanings.

## So Why All the Focus on Getting the Words Right?

We need to come back now to where we started. Why is it that, with all this complexity around words, there is still in reading instruction and research so much emphasis on reading as the correct reading of all the words? For now we can say that it stems from the difficulty people have in seeing beyond the words to the complex and dynamic ways that language represents meaning. Much of the testing of reading is focused on word accuracy often out of context. Our concern should be on making sense.

### The Brain Functions Holistically

Though we discuss this in other parts of the book, it is important here to stress why reading has to be seen holistically and why studying letter, character, or word identification can produce misunderstandings of the process.

## Going to the Largest Unit

There is a simple hierarchy which seems counter-intuitive unless you understand the efficiency with which the brain uses minimal information to get to meaning:

a book is easier to read than a chapter;
a chapter is easier to read than a page;

a page is easier to read than a paragraph;
a paragraph is easier to read than a sentence;
a sentence is easier to read then a word; and
a word is easier to read than a letter.

The larger the unit, the smaller proportion of input it takes to read it. I don't mean that a longer book is easier to read than a short one or a short story. I mean the whole is easier to read than any of its parts. And of course by *read* I mean make sense. The brain is so efficient that it selects the minimum amount of input from the text that it needs to get to the meaning.

So the rest of the cues from the text are redundant. The reader sees enough to set the pattern and the rest is redundant confirmation. This is why the redundancies resulting from the various levels of realization within language and that relate language and social interaction are so important to language processing. We need to emphasize that *redundant* does not imply unimportant. Rather, information is usually signaled through language in several ways, and therefore within a complete text there are usually multiple signals that cue the same sorts of information. (Of course, readers, in contrast to listeners, have the option to reread the text if they are truly puzzled about the meaning of a particular passage.)

## Holistic Remembering

When children begin to read, they sometimes surprise their parents by being able to remember and read a whole book themselves, page by page, after having heard it read several times. Often someone will comment, "She's not really reading, she memorized the book." It's worth noting that she didn't simply memorize all the words of the book in sequence.

Pappas and Brown (1988) studied "repeated pretend readings" by pre-reading children and demonstrated that the children developed a sense of the structure of the story they were reading. They were **not just** remembering the words and sentences of the story better.

If we took a list of all the words from the book, alphabetized them and then read the resulting list over and over to the child, would she also be able to remember and read that list? Of course not. The whole has a unity around the meaning that is easy to remember because everything supports everything else. And the enjoyment of hearing the book over and over facilitates the whole process. I call this *holistic remembering*. It plays an important role in reading development.

## FRAMES AND LOOPING

Human memory seems to be organized in such a way that things are easy to remember when we have meaningful frames to put them in. Isolated words are hard to remember but the same words are easy to remember when they are in a meaningful context. In psychological terms, these frames are schemas.

In neurological terms, the concept of looping that Steve discusses seems to offer some explanation. Each decision or action the brain controls includes a prediction of what will follow. It would have to be so. The speed at which we talk would not be possible if every decision had to be made anew. The reader has schema for organizing meaning. These are what make such smooth and rapid sequences of actions possible whether walking, reading, or driving a car. In reading we get evidence of this from the miscues readers produce.

## Schema Driven and Schema Forming Miscues

When miscues occur they are usually schema-driven, that is, the schema that produces expected responses also produces miscues. If the miscues make sense, they are unlikely to be corrected. Efficient reading avoids unneeded corrections. But some miscues are schema-forming: they happen when the reader can't fit the new input into the existing schema. Piaget calls that *disequilibrium* (Piaget, 1971). We are trying to reconcile what we have predicted with what we are getting as input but they don't match. If we can't correct by seeking more input, then we have to reconsider the schemas we have and revise them or reject them and create a new schema.

## References

Dahl, R. (1958). "Poison." In Inglis, R. B. and Spear, J. (Eds.), *Adventures in English literature* (pp. 604–611). New York: Harcourt, Brace.

Goodman, K. S. (1996). *On reading*. Portsmouth, NH: Heinemann.

Goodman, K. S. and Gespass, S. (1983). *Text features as they relate to miscues: Pronouns*. Program in Language and Literacy Occasional Paper No. 7. Program in Language and Literacy, College of Education, Room 504, University of Arizona, Tucson, AZ 85721.

Goodman, K. S. and Bird, L. B. (1984). "On the wording of texts: A study of intra-text word frequency." *Research in the Teaching of English, 18*(2), 119–145.

Halliday, M. A. K. (2004). "Three aspects of children's language development: Learning language, learning through language, learning about language." In Webster, J. (Ed.), *The language of early childhood. Volume 4 in the collected works of M.A.K. Halliday* (pp. 308–326). New York: Continuum.

Hayes, W. D. (1963). "My Brother is a Genius." In Betts, E. and Welch, C. (Eds.), *Adventures now and then* (pp. 246–256). New York: American Book Company.

Moore, L. (1965). "Freddie Miller, Scientist." In Betts, E. and Welch, C. (Eds.), *Adventures here and there* (pp. 61–68). New York: American Book Company.

O'Brien, R. C. and Bernstein, Z. (1971). *Mrs. Frisby and the rats of NIMH.* New York: Atheneum.

Pappas, C. C. and Brown, E. (1988). "The development of children's sense of the written story register: An analysis of the texture of kindergarteners' 'Pretend reading' texts." *Linguistics and Education, 1*(1), 45–79.

Perrin, S. (1976). "Declaration of Independence kit." *Visible Language, 10*(3), 253–256.

Piaget, J. (1971). *Psychology and epistemology.* New York: Grossman.

Rapoport, R. (1970). "Why we need a generation gap." *Look Magazine,* 14. January 13, 1970.

Ryan, D. (1978). "A challenge to the procedure of miscue analysis: An investigation of changes in reading behaviour." Doctoral dissertation, Monash University, Clayton, Australia.

Sperry, A. (1967). "Ghost of the Lagoon." In Robinson, H. (Ed.), *Open highways* (pp. 395–409). Glenview, IL: Scott, Foresman.

Stovall, J. (1966). "Sheep Dog." In Shel, W. and McCracken, R. (Eds.), *Widening Views, Book viii* (pp. 80–89). Boston, MA: Allyn and Bacon.

# The Visible Level of Written Language: The Graphophonic

**7**

## Whole to Part and Part to Whole

 So, I hear you asking, where is phonics in all this? I wrote a book about that called *Phonics Phacts* (Goodman, 1993). Phonics is probably the most written about and the least understood aspect of reading. Phonics is the relationship between the sound patterns (phonology) of the oral form of a language and the letter patterns (orthography) of a language with an alphabetic writing system. It is common to treat the alphabet as the final stage in the historical development of writing. That implies that all other writing systems are inferior to alphabetic ones.

But, in the modern world, there are billions of people literate in modern non-alphabetic languages, particularly Chinese and Japanese. Long before Alexander's conquests in the West, the Qing emperor in China established a single monetary, measurement, and writing system in the vast area of China. Chinese writing uses characters that represent meaning directly rather than the oral sounds so it can be understood by speakers of mutually non-understandable forms of Chinese. Long before European nations, China was thus unified.

## The Graphophonic Level of Language

Let's consider now the only observable level of written language—what we see as we read. I've called this level *graphophonic* in reading English or other alphabetic languages. There are three parts to this level:

- The phonology: this is the sound system of the language.
- The orthography: this is the complete writing system, including spelling, spacing, and punctuation.
- Phonics: the set of relationships between these two systems.

## A Definition of Phonics

Though phonics, by my definition, is an aspect of alphabetically written language, in the literature on reading, it is often used as a method of reading instruction that teaches through letter-sound relationships. We'll discuss reading instruction in our last chapter.

## Phonics: The Over-Simplification Illusion

The phonics illusion is that reading depends on the ability to sound out words. In its extreme form, it is considered the only strategy necessary. Before we consider why this is an illusion, we'll redefine phonics and discuss its real role in reading.

Above I defined phonics as the set of relationships between the sound system and the writing system in alphabetically written language. In the history of writing systems, the modern Roman alphabet and the Cyrillic (used in Russian and other Slavic language) as well as Hebrew and Arabic evolved from a single alphabet. *Alphabet* itself is a word derived from the first two letter names *alpha beta* in Greek, *aleph bet* in Hebrew. Non-alphabetic writing systems such as Chinese relate characters to concepts like numerals relate to numbers. The numeral is a sign that represents the number which is an abstract mathematical concept. And they represent the same concept no matter what they are called in a given language. The numeral 1 is *one, uno, une, eins, udine* depending on the language. Characters do not directly relate to any sounds of Chinese though some characters contain an element, rebus-like, that suggests this character represents the sound that another look-alike character does.

Oral language uses sounds as its symbols and produces them through manipulating the organs of the mouth in a time sequence. And the sound stream which the speaker has produced is received by the listener's ear which transmits signals to the brain that are then turned into perceptions. The symbols are actually not single sounds but phonemes, ranges of sounds which are perceived by users of the language as a particular phoneme. So each sound influences what comes before and after.

## Phonemes

Phonemes are perceptual illusions. For example, say the words latter and ladder. Depending on your dialect, they will either sound the same or you will perceive a clear difference. Again, what you think you hear is more important than what you actually hear. In all aspects of language learning, what not to pay attention to is as important as what to pay attention to. That's why in learning English, Japanese speakers have trouble perceiving the difference between *late* and *rate* or why English listeners heard *Peking* when Chinese speakers told them the city was *Beijing*.

Remarkably, the brain adjusts for the influences of the changes in sounds depending on what precedes and follows them to the extent that we "hear" sounds which aren't actually there. Phoneticians, using very precise acoustic instruments, have demonstrated that what reaches the ear and what people describe as what they hear are often quite different.

Written language is produced on a two-dimensional space. It is displayed across that space in a horizontal or vertical direction. Modern Chinese and Japanese can be written either horizontally or vertically.

## Graphemes

A written letter, linguists would call it a *grapheme*, is an abstract form realized by a wide range of fonts. It is also a perceptual unit. There are no dependable single features of a letter common to all ways of writing it. Look at this row of Gs for example G, ɡ, **ɡ**, **g**, g, **G**, ɡ, *G*, $g$, **G**, G, **g**, G, *G*, g. Yet we treat these very different forms as the same. Now add to this that those g words would have sounded different in different dialects. The letters <ng> in words such as *singer*, *Long Island* represent a single sound /ŋ/ in some English dialects, but some speakers produce two sounds /ŋg/ in those words. Most speakers

Not all variation is ambiguity. Two issues are involved: 1. Variation in form with a single interpretation—a letter (G) is really an abstract sign with a variety of realizations. 2. A single sign that may be interpreted in more than one way. For linguists, *ambiguity* addresses the latter issue. The variation of the shapes of <g> addresses the first. Now consider these words spelled with g: *Wag, wage, edge, ghost, light, laugh, grind, fragile, though, beige, sing, singe.* Here we see our set for ambiguity at work but this time the symbol changes value in these words. Things that look the same can be treated as different. The abstract letter <g> fits a range of sounds. But letter <u>patterns</u> represent patterns of sound. Ambiguity is in the shapes that letters take and a great deal of variation in how <u>English spelling patterns</u> relate to the sound patterns of the oral language.

of English alternate their pronunciations of words such as *walking, teaching,* and *coming*, sometimes using an /ŋ/ (particularly in more formal contexts) and producing /n/ (often written *walkin', teachin',* and *comin'*) in informal contexts. But the spelling stays the same.

## Personal Phonics

How many ways have you heard these words pronounced: *almond, apricot, ceiling, roof, room, root, fog, dog, log, bog, caught, cot.* Do *Mary, merry,* and *marry* sound the same or different? So how can there be *a* single phonics for all dialects of American English. The short answer is that there isn't. We have to modify our definition of phonics:

> Phonics is the set of relationships between **a speaker's phonology** and the **orthography** of the language.

Each of us, within the dialect(s) we control, has our own phonics. In standardizing the spelling, the printers intuitively knew that readers of a wide range of dialects would be able to make sense of the books. But each reader, in the context of the wording (lexicogrammar) and the meaning (semantics), uses a personal set of phonics relationships.

## Ambiguity and Redundancy in Using Phonics

With the complex spelling system of English phonics, even your personal phonics could only get you to a possible pronunciation of a word. But with the other information available, the set for ambiguity and the redundancy are at work and the readers can have a sense of what the term or phrase means even if they can't be sure of the pronunciation. If the personal phonics in context produces something close enough to a term the readers find familiar that fits the meaning, then they may correct to the actual term as they pronounce it. Our miscue research is full of such examples.

In *FM* (Moore, 1965) the words *chemistry, chemist, chemical,* and *chemicals* appear several times. One subject pronounced *chemistry* with a ch /č/ sound when it modified a noun but got *chemist* and *chemistry* right when they were head nouns in their phrases.

In another story, *My Brother Is a Genius* (Hayes, 1963), the word *typical* occurs ten times referring to a baby who is supposed to be typical but turns out not to be. In our research study, 32 subjects read the story. Eight of the 32 read *typical* correctly the first time. One or two subjects didn't attempt to say it. On each occurrence from 8–13 readers produced other real words instead of *typical*: these were *tropical, topical, tricycle, tropic,* and one instance *testicle*. That shows they were trying to think of possible words they knew. Most stuck to this reading across the occurrences. About an equal number of subjects produced non-word pronunciations. Most common was *typeical* using a "long I" by 9 subjects. Those mostly stayed with that. Others tended to make different attempts unsuccessfully.

## Real World Use of Phonics

The common-sense view of phonics as "sounding out" is not how phonics actually is used. The strategy is more like:

1.  Try some attempt at what the word might sound like: typeical is a pretty good first try.
2.  Think of how that word might look and/or sound and fit with the grammar and meaning contexts.
3.  Try other possibilities.
4.  Use a real word or a non-word as a place holder if you aren't able to get a word that fits.

Phonics gets the reader an approximation which can be enough if the term is familiar as it was with about a third of these subjects. For the others, they can get some sense of the meaning even if they don't get the word. With all this variation, most subjects showed in their retellings some sense that *typical* meant something like average.

## Seven, Plus or Minus Two

George Miller (1956), who brought linguistics into psychology, did some studies that came up with a famous insight. The brain can perceive and remember seven plus or minus two items the eye sees for a split second. That led me to develop a demonstration I often used to show how what the brain brings to the perception determines how much we can see at a glance. I called this the Lines of Print. I would flash on a screen a line of print and ask my audience to write down everything they could remember seeing. The lines varied.

The first line I projected was this:

**1.**  ⊏◁ ○ ◇ ◫ ⁂ ✳ △ ◻ ◁ ◘ 8

Figure 7.1 Geometric Figures

With these vaguely geometric figures, the audience could remember only a few and they could not reproduce them accurately. Was that bottom line flat or at an angle?

**2.** **67495386479012**

**3.** **azqrdgfdeomslp**

Figure 7.2 Numerals and Letters

In the lines that showed numerals or letters, people seemed to know the category—numerals, for example, before they identified them. That seems strange. Don't you have to identify them before you can assign them to a category? Knowing the category is apparently necessary to recognizing the individual characters.

One line looked like this:

**149162536496481**

Most people could only remember the first three to five numerals. They usually could not remember whether they saw a closed 4 or open 4 so they wrote the one they usually write. But a few people could reproduce the whole line. That's because they saw a pattern in this line. Do you see a pattern? Hint: Think math. Think squares.

The one line that almost everybody "saw" completely was:

**Can you read this?**

But only an occasional person could do the same thing with this:

אנ ׳ י ׳ כו ל ׳ לקרא עברית

**Figure 7.3** Hebrew

Those who were successful knew Hebrew so they knew it said (in Hebrew) "I can read in Hebrew." Other readers could remember fewer characters than even the vague shapes and they were at the wrong end of the line since Hebrew is read from right to left.

## Vision and Perception

This demonstration shows two related things about perception as compared to vision:

1.  It is not what the eye sees in each instance that varies—it's what the observer knows. With the same amount of time to gather visual input,

my audience could remember "seeing" a whole meaningful line but only a few letters or numerals and even fewer abstract figures.

2. That means known wholes are perceived more easily than their components. In reading, as in all aspects of knowing, the brain is constantly matching input with what it already knows. In fact, we see parts from the whole not the whole from the parts. Linguists talk about "distinctive features." In looking at print, we must certainly leap to the whole from the same features that we would use to identify a letter, a numeral, a character, or a word. But we also have the context of grammar and wording. With the focus on making sense in reading, we can perceive a whole short sentence as efficiently as a letter or word, even when that sentence is beyond what the eye can see in a single fixation.

So Miller's seven plus or minus two expands depending on how much the reader knows. This is part of the explanation for the grand illusion, of course. Our brains make such efficient use of visual input that we leap to meaning and then we are sure we have seen it all.

I learned something else from using the lines of print quite accidentally. I had numbered the lines with a line number and period before each line. But no one ever included the number in what he or she wrote down. In fact, most people could not remember whether the lines were numbered. They had repressed any recognition of the line number in focusing on the task of writing what they remembered reading. This is an example of what some have called *selective attention*. The people who participated in these exercises focused on the things they considered to be relevant and ignored the other factors that seemed to them to be irrelevant.

## Using the Minimum of Phonics

There are many implications for understanding how the brain uses what it knows to get the most knowledge from the minimum of visual clues. Everyone has some words in their vocabulary that they more or less understand but mispronounce. One for me was *victuals*. That was a word I found in Dickens but I thought I hadn't heard it. It was only when an author complained to me that his editor didn't like his character saying, *"Hey, Ma are the victuals ready?"* that I realized *victuals* is pronounced *vittles*.

## Invented Spellings

There is a body of research that shows that young children learning to read and write do develop their personal phonics. Research on invented spelling demonstrates that. As children begin to write, they like to write their names and will sometimes begin to use those same letters to pretend to spell other words. They start to notice as they read and see print in their environment how the words are spelled. This leads to invented spellings as they experiment with producing spellings. In general, these invented spellings show the personal phonics they are developing.

One thing that each child has to learn is that this personal phonics only gets them in the neighborhood and they need the rest of the context to get the wording. It should be obvious that encouraging kids to think about how words are spelled can help this process; teaching them a set of specific letter-sound relationships may actually inhibit the process.

The key thing to understand is that the three kinds of information (graphophonic, lexicogrammatical, and semantic) that readers use as they construct meaning support each other in the particular context—both linguistic and social—where the reading occurs. The information is used selectively and simultaneously. Where there is ambiguity in spelling, word meaning, or syntax, the systems provide redundant information to help readers disambiguate what they see. This process of making sense of print is consistent with how the brain constructs meaning.

Encountering an unfamiliar phrase or word or something familiar but used in an unfamiliar way, the reader can still make sense if the context created by the other systems narrows the possible meaning. And with the universal set for ambiguity just enough phonics can bring to mind a word which looks like what we see and sounds like it might fit the meaning and wording context.

Leland Jacobs, a great authority on children's literature and reading at Teachers' College, Columbia University, liked to paraphrase an old hair product commercial: "Phonics—a little dab'll do you" (personal communication, 1967).

## Punctuation

Punctuation in written language serves a purpose that is very similar to the function of intonation, but punctuation is not nearly as complete a system. In oral language, we can string together a long series of clauses and the intonation, rhythm, and stress lets our listeners know how the clauses relate to each other. In writing, we can put periods at the ends of sentences and use commas, colons, and semicolons to indicate boundaries of various structures.

Though punctuation helps, we usually use much shorter sentences in writing than in speech to help our readers interpret what we say.

## *Space as Punctuation*

Another type of "punctuation" is the use of space sometimes called "layout."

In written language, the use of spacing is one of the most important ways of making a text comprehensible. Just look at any page of a magazine or a newspaper to see how important spacing is. A good page to look at is the editorial or op-ed page of any newspaper. Notice how the various items are spaced. There may be a cartoon. How do the editors separate one item—a lead editorial for example—from the rest of the items on the page? It may fill the width of two columns. Other items may be across the bottom spanning all the columns. Or an item may be set apart in a text box.

The editor lets you know the relative importance through several devices:

- amount of space devoted to it;
- choice of font and font size; and
- headlines may be large font and bold face.

But look carefully at how white space is used. Paragraphs can be indented or there may be an extra line of white space between paragraphs. Too much text without space in between may make the page uninviting. There is a rule of journalism that the writer must put the important information first and the detail last.

The systems at all levels work together. What we've been showing here is that natural language works in ways that support its use in human communication. The systems support each other. In learning to understand oral language as young children, we learn to use the cues of language to make sense. So, too, we learn to use our knowledge of language to make sense of print.

There is an understandable tendency to try to make the texts we use to teach reading simpler for young learners. But any attempt to do so by manipulating or tampering with the language by use of controlled vocabulary, controlling spelling patterns, or limiting phonics sequences makes the language unnatural and therefore less predictable for the reader. And so it is more likely to impede reading development rather than facilitate.

## Readability

Over the years, various "readability formulas" have sought to find ways of quantifying the reading difficulty of written-language texts. They have looked at factors such as sentence and word length, grammatical complexity, use of uncommon words, and so on. While these formulas may have some validity in comparing texts, their use to rewrite or simplify texts is likely to make the texts unnatural. A version may be produced which has a lower readability score—but in the process the text has been made less predictable and therefore harder and not easier.

## References

Goodman, K. S. (1993). *Phonics phacts*. Richmond Hill, ON: Scholastic Canada.

Hayes, W. D. (1963). "My brother is a genius." In Betts, E. and Welch, C. (Eds.), *Adventures now and then* (pp. 246–256). New York: American Book Company.

Miller, G. A. (1956). "The magical number seven, plus or minus two: Some limits on our capacity for processing information." *Psychological Review, 63*(2), 81–97.

Moore, L. (1965). "Freddie Miller, Scientist." In Betts, E. and Welch, C. (Eds.), *Adventures here and there* (pp. 61–68). New York: American Book Company.

# Literacy for the Twenty-First Century and Beyond

8

 A central goal of this book has been to share our understanding of how reading works—how readers make sense of and through written language. Our focus has been on reading and literacy. In understanding how reading works, we have offered insights into how the brain works and of the central relationships of language and thought. We've also seen how reading is, in fact, an instantiation of the dynamic ways the brain works in general. The book said a lot about how our brains are able to transcend the limits of our senses and about the illusions the brain creates that are vital in constructing representations of the world around us to make it possible to navigate our way around the real world safely and efficiently.

## Focus on Learning

Now we shift our focus to how we learn to read. The common-sense view of learning to read is that it is rather difficult to learn but an important ability that is necessary for success in school and life. In this final chapter, we hope you will come to revalue learning to read and to revalue how teaching supports that learning. If we have succeeded, you now see reading as making sense of print which is a natural extension of making sense of speech. We are using the term revalue because it implies not simply having a new understanding of what it means to become literate but also a new appreciation of this remarkable human personal and social achievement.

## Learning to Read and Write Is Easy

Everything we've said in this book leads us to believe that written language should be easier to learn than oral language. That's because the strategies needed to understand and make oneself understood in written language are basically the same ones already learned for oral language. And two of the three language systems—the wording (lexicogrammar) and the semantic (meaning) system are essentially the same for oral and written language. It follows then that becoming readers and writers should happen as a natural extension of oral language when it is needed by communities and by the individuals in them. That also means that the same universal ability to develop oral language works equally well with written language.

## *What Reading Is, How it Is Learned, and How Teaching Relates to Each*

Reading is a form of language parallel to listening. For speakers of a language individually and collectively, written language becomes necessary when it is needed to connect with others beyond immediate face-to-face context. So written language is learned for the same reasons and in much the same way as oral language. However, there is a common belief that written language is a kind of code for oral language which makes it more difficult to learn and which requires reading and writing to be taught as school subjects.

Some authorities believe the main task is learning how to read words. This belief suggests that reading must ultimately involve accurate word identification which they believe is necessary for comprehension. For others, ability to "crack the code," that is, to turn print into oral language is necessary, so they believe that learning to read must be the result of learning phonics.

All of these views lead to the practice of **teaching reading and writing as school subjects**. So the teaching of reading and writing more or less precedes using them for getting information or pleasure. If reading and writing are taught as school subjects, there must be some sequence of what has to be learned and in what order. In extreme forms, this sequence of skills or components is seen as so intrinsic to learning to read that it becomes reading itself and each step must absolutely be mastered or the whole is in jeopardy. Serious research is conducted on how to teach vocabulary, phonemic awareness—even on the sequence of teaching the letters of the alphabet. What makes language easy to learn is that it is encountered in its use as language—not as abstract parts of language.

The view of learning to read as learning to get the words right led to the dominance of controlled vocabulary basal readers. The sequence in the instruction was the control of the vocabulary. By the early 1920s, Thorndike and others did studies of word frequency on the theory that the most frequent words were the ones needed to be taught first (Thorndike, 1931). From about 1932, in the United States, until about 1990, controlled vocabulary *basal reading programs* became dominant. They used little artificial stories to teach the words. Phonics was one of several *word attack skills*.

Throughout that time, there were strong proponents of phonics who characterized non-phonics basals as *Look-say* to ridicule the notion that one could read words without sounding them out by applying phonics rules that were learned in advance. So, the sequence was controlled introduction of letter-sound relationships.

At the present time, more extreme forms of phonics have become popular with politicians and in the U.S. have been written into the "No Child Left Behind" law. In England, the political question is whether analytic or synthetic phonics should be mandated. There are many variations of these two views but from our perspective they both are based on two false premises. First is that written language is harder to learn than oral language and therefore must be taught as a school subject. Second, that it is possible to establish a defensible sequence to teach reading and writing that does not require children to learn rules and *skills* which have questionable validity, result in strange and artificial texts, and are harder to learn than it is to learn to read.

## A Bold Proposal

From what we have learned about reading, we want to state the case for a bold proposal:

**Reading and writing should not be taught as school subjects to be learned parallel to math, science, social studies, and the arts. Instead, literacy should be learned in the process of its use. The learning will happen:**

1.  **If the learners see reading and writing as necessary to connect with others.**
2.  **If the learners are participants in a culture in which written language is used to connect.**

## Nothing New

This is not a new idea. Here's what Vygotsky said:

> The best method (for teaching reading and writing) is one in which children do not learn to read and write but in which both these skills are found in play situations. . . . In the same way as children learn to speak, they should be able to learn to read and write.
>
> (Cole, John-Steiner, Scribner and Sauberman, 1978: 118)

Frank Smith (1973) contrasted how easy it is to make learning to read difficult and how hard it is to make it easy.

Twelve easy ways to make learning to read difficult and one difficult way to make it easy:

1.  Aim for early mastery of the rules of reading.
2.  Ensure that phonic skills are learned and used.
3.  Teach letters or words one at a time, making sure each new letter or word is learned before moving on.
4.  Make word-perfect reading the prime objective.
5.  Discourage guessing; be sure children read carefully.
6.  Insist upon accuracy.
7.  Provide immediate feedback.
8.  Detect and correct inappropriate eye movements.
9.  Identify and give special attention to problem readers as soon as possible.
10. Make sure children understand the importance of reading and the seriousness of falling behind.
11. Take the opportunity during reading instruction to improve spelling and written expression, and also insist on the best possible spoken English.
12. If the method you are using is unsatisfactory, try another. Always be alert for new materials and techniques.

(p. 185)

Smith's one hard way to make learning to read easy:

1. Respond to what the child is trying to do.

## Connecting

What the child is doing is trying to connect through reading and writing. In this book, we have said repeatedly: every human has the ability to use abstract systems of signs to represent how we perceive the world and represent our ideas of that world to ourselves and to each other. I am using *connect* rather than *communicate* because this need to connect goes far beyond communication. Communication is very important but nothing melts the heart of a parent more than the first *I wuv you* from a two year old. Through language we connect ourselves to our loved ones, to our cultures, to our heritage. We connect to belong.

Most children are introduced to their culture through songs, folktales, and family lore at early ages. One important reason for the development of written language is to store and pass on to future generations the culture of a community including its religious teachings and beliefs, its laws and traditions, and its stories, poetry, and history. And in recent decades we are finding ways of connecting that exceed the confines of time and space.

## Invention and Convention

The language inventions we each produce are constrained by the conventions of the social language used by family and friends in connecting with us. There is then an internal force on language development which is countered by the social constraint of conventions and eventually these two forces come into balance more or less and our personal language conforms to the social. This tension between invention and convention also results in some of the change that happens over time in the social language.

What is most remarkable about this process is that each of us achieves control of one or more oral languages at a very early age without any explicit instruction. Language is so universally achieved that it seems as natural as each of us getting up on our two feet and walking. There is overwhelming evidence that the developing human mind finds language learning easy. Not only does it not require any high degree of intelligence but it seems unlimited—infants learn whatever languages they need to connect with those around them. It is not uncommon for children in Africa, for example, to know three or more languages that they need before they are four or five years old. It is sufficient for a child to be around people who are connecting with each other through any language for the language to be learned. That's true for every language. That's true for every form of language.

There is indeed something uniquely and universally human about this remarkable achievement of creating symbolic systems for connecting with each other so that we can share what we need, what we experience, what we learn and understand. Language in all its forms multiplies the human intelligence of any one individual because we can learn through language what others have learned. Our human relationships—families, clans, communities, and nations—are built largely through language. And the more complex our human need to connect with each other, the more powerful ways we find for connecting over time and space and circumstance. We govern ourselves through language. We express our most profound and most intimate thoughts and create great beauty through language.

## Thinking Symbolically Makes Language Easy to Learn

What makes language possible is that the human brain thinks symbolically and so learning a language is easy because it fits the way we think. Who would ever suggest that there would be an advantage to subjecting infants to a curriculum of skill drills and talking lessons over letting them learn to talk? Yet in school for centuries instead of making literacy a natural extension of language development, we turned learning to read and write into a subject to be learned bit by bit until it was learned well enough to use in reading and writing to learn.

## What We Propose

**We propose that the way to put to work the universal ability of children to learn to read and write easily is to support it happening in the context of the functional need to connect through written language.**

## The Digital Natives

And, in fact, a digital revolution is producing kids who have learned to read and write as easily as they learned to talk. Kids two, three, and four years old are connecting with other kids their own age with a device that uses print. Connecting through that device they easily learn to read and write, at very early ages, as they learned to text and use email—without instruction—before they come to school.

Quite a few young children have been learning without instruction even before the new devices. And the vast majority of kids growing up in print-rich environments know a lot about written language before they start school:

• Growing up in a print-rich environment, one of the first things they begin to respond to are familiar logos and signs. They recognize fast food stores and brand names.

• Observing and participating in literacy uses in the family:
    – notes on their doors: Kepe awt. Mnstr;
    – refrigerator notice boards;
    – emails, texting, note writing;
    – games and songs;
    – television, videos, apps on iPads and smart phones; and
    – their own names and those of family members.

In some cultures, Japan particularly, it's pretty much the norm for children to be reading when they enter school. Millions of copies of pre-school magazines are sold in Japan and "education mamas" read them with their kids.

But now—think about how widespread text messaging has become. Anybody, child or adult, with access to a cell phone can engage in a written conversation with someone in the next seat or across the room or across the world in any language. Social networks make it easy to connect with *friends* on a computer, a phone, or an iPad. In the digital world, readers and writers alternate roles as they do in oral language. That has profoundly changed the social context that facilitates learning to read and write, making it much more like oral language. So literacy is happening as a natural extension of language development and it is likely that many more children are learning written language at the very same time that they are learning oral language and in much the same way. That way is by participation. In the process of connecting with those immediately around us, we learn to talk and to understand speech. So we learn, again quoting Frank Smith (1988), *by joining the literacy club*, by connecting on the internet (by friending), texting on the cell phone, or playing a computer game that responds to our typed commands.

Both the children who learned to read on their own and the new group of digital natives are demonstrating the remarkable and universal language learning ability of our species. Young humans are universally able to learn language in the course of using it.

That need to connect is what is driving the digital revolution among young people. It is the human need to connect that creates the technology and not the other way around. I've said earlier that the common belief that Gutenberg's printing press led to popular literacy is wrong. The growing need for widespread literacy made his printing press possible. It answered the demand for multiple copies of books, and opened up the possibilities of what followed as more people became literate—magazines, newspapers, flyers, etc.

Now generations of copiers, computers, smart phones, and all of the derivatives are becoming obsolete before their users have had time to learn how to use them fully. They are responding to the ever-increasing need for instantaneous connecting across space and to the need for easy access to information. The important thing is not technology itself that is the breakthrough—it is the literacy it makes possible. In fact, there is a strong tendency to miss that and to harness the technology to old curricula and methodology.

## LEARNING THROUGH TEXTING

There is one feature of the technology of text messages and email that particularly facilitates learning written language. In other forms of reading and writing, there is separation of the roles of reader and writer. The author writes and then mails the letter or publishes it. The reader is somewhere else at another time. But in digital media, reader and writer are chatting or quickly responding to each other's message. In fact, the word *chat* is borrowed from oral language because of its similarity to the informality and quick give and take. This is, of course, exactly like oral language—with the exception that participants can't usually see each other (unless they are skyping, of course). The quick responses make development of written language a much easier transition from the oral language development the learners have already achieved.

## Achieving in School What Children are Already Achieving Outside of School

Our bold proposal should also not be that new for successful teachers. Good teachers have always intuited that children are good at learning language and have attempted to attend to and build on their language learning ability, even when the official literacy curriculum was not conducive to that.

It's not my intention to provide a fully developed curriculum for implementing learning literacy through its use, but here are propositions that it can be based on:

### Proposition 1

*Language exists always in the context of its use. That's the way it has to be experienced for anyone to make sense of it. So anything the learner is expected to read in or out of school has to have all the characteristics of real language.* It can't be doctored up, chopped up, or dumbed down to fit a skill sequence. Language is no longer language if it is broken into word lists, lists of unrelated sentences, or phonics drills. Everything supports everything else as long as it is real language.

### Proposition 2

*Anything a child is asked to read in school or out has to have value and function for that child* (not something to be learned because it will be needed in the future). The reason why kids are texting and emailing is because they are able to participate in a way of connecting with others as part of popular social practice. Expanding on their use of literacy depends on their need to make use of the new forms or aspects of language in order to participate.

### Proposition 3

*The learner must be valued as a language learner.* That means valuing the dialects and languages he or she already has learned. And it means the culture of the learner must be valued. All children coming to school have successfully learned the most important forms of language for them: those of their family and community. And they can build literacy on the same base. Correcting what is considered by some a non-standard dialect while they are learning to read confuses them and inhibits their learning.

## Proposition 4

***THERE ARE NO PREREADING SKILLS, SIGHT WORDS, OR RULES THAT MUST BE LEARNED PRIOR TO LEARNING IN GENERAL OR AS PREPARA-TION FOR ANY NEW ACTIVITY.*** There is no need for "readiness activities." The culture of teaching written language as a school subject is so ingrained that it makes it seem like there has to be something that needs to be learned outside of language before it can be learned. Don't they need to know the alphabet? Shouldn't they know words before they can read them? They surely need to learn some phonics rules?

The answer is no to all of the above. We do not learn language from part to whole. Language is learned by participating in its use. We learn what we need to know as we use the language and talk about it. We learn about language while we learn language by learning through language as Michael Halliday (2004) has observed.

## Proposition 5

*The literacy already achieved must be valued and welcomed in the classroom.* Any assignments and activities must include use of this literacy. Start where the learner is. That's one of John Dewey's (1938) most important teachings. There needs to be continuity so children can expand on the base they have achieved. Just as their language must be accepted, so must their forms of literacy. The goal is not to replace but to accept, build, and expand on what they can do.

## Proposition 6

*Every activity or experience in school and out is an opportunity to support the expansion of literacy.* This is the key to developing literacy through using it. Words have no meaning except in the contexts in which they are experienced and to make sense of language all systems have to be present. The time to learn to make sense of and learn through new genres, new functions, is as they are encountered in using them.

## SOME EXAMPLES:

The first experiences young children have with written language is in print-rich communities in which they live. They associate logos with stores, become aware of street signs, and their parents' uses of written language. If their parents tell stories and read to them, they come to have a sense of story structure and how print represents meaning. For some, this exposure is enough to start them reading. The ease at which they take control of digital devices is a perfect example of learning through participation.

So it should be in school. Every school experience is an opportunity to learn the language necessary to participate. The genius of the teacher is to be aware of what children already know, what interests them, to involve them in fruitful experiences and talk about language, and to know how to monitor their development.

- As the learner is writing a sign for the hamster cage, she is becoming aware of the function of environmental literacy.
- While the learner focuses on math problems, there is an opportunity to learn to translate practical math problems into operations or to use language to express math algorithms and vice versa. The child is learning to use language to learn math; the teacher is monitoring both.
- The learner is gathering information for a group presentation on migratory birds. The teacher brainstorms with the group. Then they use books and internet to gather information.

## Proposition 7

*Reading is learned by reading and writing is learned by writing and each supports the other.* In research on miscue analysis, we found that every reader is learning every time he or she reads. As Margaret Meek Spencer (1987) puts it, "texts teach." And not all reading has to be in books. Print is everywhere—even on television screens. Maximizing time spent reading and writing (for real purposes) should be the major concern of educators.

## Proposition 8

*To err is human and a vital part of learning. All attempts must be honored.* When literacy is developing (and isn't it always?), it contains miscues, approximations, and inventions. There is a time for editing what will be published or shared with an audience such as a letter, a presentation, or a publication. But as in learning to talk, correction inhibits; positive response encourages.

Any lessons on aspects of written language should come out of the real use of language and go back into it. There are times when it is useful for teachers to call the attention of one or more pupils to some characteristic of language that is causing some difficulty or is of particular interest. Invented spelling is a good example of the role of error in learning. It's natural for language learners to look for patterns and rules. So when a young child writes *wuz* for *was* it shows an attempt to use personal phonics—it could be a spelling. That's good. But in developing phonics rules, the learner has to also be aware that they only get you close. Spelling is learned primarily through reading but that works best if the learner also writes regularly. That's because in reading the writer notes how a word he or she needs in writing looks. Oh, it's *were* not *wur*. If the learner has inferred a rule, it will be modified through experience.

If rules are taught before they are needed, they are:

1.   Hard to learn.
2.   Hard to stop using, even if they don't work.

What is important: keep the learner in charge of the learning and think through what literacy is involved in each planned experience. The teacher is the coach or mediator. Corrections or grades are much less useful than supporting comments or questions.

## And a Motto for the Kids: When in Doubt, Figure it Out!

In sum what I'm saying is simple: literacy has been made hard to learn by treating it as a new subject. It has become easier with the widespread natural development into digital literacy. Schools need to work with the learners to use their universal language learning ability.

## Connecting to Culture

The purpose of language education in school is to expand on what the learners have already achieved. That means building on their interest in stories and offering opportunities to explore forms of literature. It means using their interest in songs to explore poetry.

When I talk about learning through use, that includes the use of literature in all the forms in which it appears. To be full participants in society, we need to connect with our culture. And schools need to catch up with the ways in which this is happening. Books are still important but there are alternative forms in which literature is available. Ours is a multimedia world and education needs to keep up.

## Time for Language Development

So much time is currently spent on teaching reading and writing as subjects that it often crowds out everything else including reading and writing for any personal purposes. And there is little time for talk. That's because time is devoted to learning the skill sequence, practicing, and being tested on the assumed components.

When part of the day is devoted to reading, it should be time to read books of the students own choice, to share responses to a book, author, or theme through a literature study group, or in the early grades to share reading a big book. Time is devoted to silent reading and similarly there should be time devoted to writing but writing for a personal purpose: to keep a journal, create a story, poem, or play, or responding to an experience or inquiry. And there should be support in using the appropriate forms of reading and writing throughout the school day during all the subject areas using whatever devices are most facilitative. The best way to practice reading and writing is to do a lot of it while using it for a real purpose. If it seems I'm being redundant in saying this, it's because schools have for so long thought of the actual reading and writing as practicing the component skills, not supporting students in its authentic uses.

In secondary schools, every teacher is a reading and writing teacher. There are forms and uses of language particular to each subject. The teacher needs to make sure that there are activities related to what is being learned that provide reasons to use a particular language form or genre. The best time to learn how to write a letter is when there is a need for one. The best time to learn how to use a reference source is when particular information is needed to find something out/answer questions raised by the student.

## *The Double Agenda*

Here's where the double agenda comes in. The teacher is noting what is being learned and is also aware of the language learning. The students are discovering the forms of language they need and are ready for support in using them. And there is time for the students to participate in both kinds of learning. There is a double payoff to the use of time because learning language and learning through language happen together.

There is also a time to study language as an interesting aspect of life. In a film made in Australia, seventh graders did a study of language difference in their community. They interviewed a union organizer, a department store manager, a disc jockey, and others. They also examined differences in their own classroom.

In a primary school in Tucson, one of the teachers organized a group to study the ways they use language in conflict resolution. The children then used what they learned to settle conflicts in their school.

## The Role of the Teacher

Don't misunderstand when we say we should stop teaching reading and writing as school subjects. We don't mean that the teacher has no role in literacy development. Quite the contrary, the teacher is the "kid watcher" who knows by observing learners what they can do and what support they need to expand their literacy (Goodman and Wilde, 1996). The teacher's role is to create situations and opportunities that make expanded literacy necessary and useful. And the teacher's job is to arrange the resources and materials for developing literacy. In this era of marginalization of knowledge, the teacher must be an advocate for the kids who are suffering under inappropriate programs and methods.

If children haven't experienced stories and books at home, then expanding digital literacy to books and other print and building enjoyment of stories is what teachers will do. Teachers must be given the recognition they deserve as professionals and they must demand that their knowledge be respected. Even the best program can't succeed without committed and knowledgeable teachers who know how to support the learners. Teachers are the professionals who know that there isn't any more reason to expect children to produce written language which is perfectly formed than it would be to expect children to sound like accomplished orators when they are learning to talk. There are ways where teachers as kid watchers can note points where a pupil could use a little help while at the same time helping that child to value what he/she can do.

The kids themselves can judge whether they do or don't understand if we encourage them to accept that reading is all about making sense. I learned long ago, first as a parent and then as a teacher, to respond to a child's question about language by first finding out the purpose of the question. Often "what does ____ mean?" is asked because the child has heard or seen some word combination in a new context and it didn't fit what he/she thought it meant. The best response to a language question is: "What do you think ____ means?" Or better still "Can you figure it out yourself?" That says to the child. "You've got strategies. Use them."

## When Instruction Conflicts with Learning

Young people don't stop learning language because they're taught. And many learn regardless of instruction. But for some students while trying to use what they are being taught, they begin to realize that what they are doing doesn't make much sense. So they may begin to use their own strategies but think they are cheating when they do so. The problem is aggravated by tests that are based on the view of reading as an autonomous process which can be taught prior to its use. The tests scores are reified and reported as representing reading ability.

Educators invented tests to help ourselves evaluate what we were doing and what the students were learning. And we oversold them to the public and to politicians. One kind of test is called *norm referenced*. As the test is being developed, it is piloted with groups of kids at each grade. The average score of the kids at a particular grade is labeled grade level. Since grade level is the average score, that means half of those who took the test will be at or above grade level and the other half will be at or below grade level. Unfortunately, when people heard us talk about grade level, they thought it meant what a kid should be able to do when he or she is in that grade. So then they said, "Oh my goodness, half those kids are reading below grade level." Human beings vary in every respect. Schools organize students by grades. But in every grade there will be a range and as children progress, the differences get wider. In language, as in everything else, the goal is growth. But that is always relative.

The tests have become more part of the problem than of any use to the teacher. A professional teacher can judge how effective a young reader is. Teachers observe children with professional knowledge and judge them by what they do when they read and how they use reading to comprehend and to learn.

Here is the central issue in measuring growth in reading and writing or in any aspect of language: *language can only be judged by how well the user is able to use it to understand or to be understood in a given context.*

Too often the history of education is lost and we begin to regard common practice as the only way to do something. So the best of reading programs are still conceived as teaching reading and writing as school subjects alongside other subjects, such as math, science, arts, and social studies. That treats reading and writing as ends in themselves and takes them out of the context of their use. By doing that, we destroy the condition that makes language easy for all humans to learn: that it is a means to connecting with others. And in taking it out of the context of its use it ceases to be language. By reifying (turning it into the reality of reading), the mastery of their skill sequence as reading each piece in the sequence becomes a prerequisite for the next. So if the sequence begins with the teaching of the alphabet then being able to pass a test on letter recognition means the student has learned a part of reading. And so not passing such a test means that the young learner cannot go on to the next part, matching letters to sounds, because that requires knowledge of the alphabet.

But as we've said, young children are very good at learning language but vary considerably in their ability to deal with abstraction. And that leads to considerable difficulty for many children in achieving a high enough score to pass from each stage of the sequence to the next. So then they get more intense instruction. Ironically, then, the instructional program produces the very literacy crisis it is designed to prevent. Under "No Child Left Behind," this extreme approach to teaching reading as a school subject was written into law and is mandated in a number of states.

## Whole Language

Beginning in the late 1960s, movements began in Britain, Australia, Canada, and the United States which were based on growing understandings of language and reading development and shifted away from the skill-based reading curriculum to a meaning-centered one. In England, the *Bullock Report*, *A Language for Life* (Bullock, 1975) emphasized every school having a language policy which recognized accepting and building on the language of the learner. Australia also emphasized learning to read for meaning.

But it was in Western Canada that teachers began to call what they were doing *whole language*. They were explicitly rejecting imported versions of the test and text methodology of the U.S. as they saw it. Instead, they were building on the developing knowledge that the reading process was making sense and on the importance of learning language through using it.

Very quickly, whole language was passing from teacher to teacher in the U.S. and coming into their classrooms. My small book, *What's Whole in Whole*

*Language* (Goodman, 1986) sold 250,000 copies in several languages—which gives some sense of how widely whole language spread.

It takes two different words to express in Spanish what the "whole" means: *integral* (complete) and *integrado* (integrated). So language is always kept whole in the context of its use and integrated with the content being studied.

What made this movement possible was the large number of professional teachers who understood and became committed to it. Unlike earlier progressive movements, whole language had a staunch group of advocates among classroom teachers and they were making it work. And make no mistake, it was attacked because it worked not because it didn't work. Too many kids of all kinds were learning too well.

## Unhappy Paradox

What a paradox: on the one hand, here are the digital natives happily texting and emailing their way into literacy ready for knowledgeable teachers to support them in the myriad opportunities a rich school experience can afford for them to use their developing literacy to learn while expanding their literacy competence. On the other hand, here are the schools they are entering where teachers are limited to being technicians administering a program based on abstractions that are in no way enabling learners to use both their developing literacy and their universal ability to learn functional and authentic whole language easily.

What is even worse than cancelling out the universal language learning ability of children in literacy development is what the obsessive imposition of the critical need to teach the skills of reading has done to the curriculum. Kindergarten has been transformed from its role as transition from home to school with a curriculum built around learning through play to a sweatshop for reading instruction.

## Manufactured Crisis

Now let's consider what the reality is for literacy in the United States and elsewhere. Is there a crisis that warrants the extremes that schools are being pushed to? I hear my readers say: everybody knows there is a serious literacy problem in this country. Lots of kids can't read at grade level. Our prisons are full of illiterates. Not!

There is no crisis in literacy. What appears to be a crisis has been called a "manufactured crisis" (Berliner and Biddle, 1995). There are no illiterate high school graduates. The crisis is manufactured for political purposes to support a campaign to make it appear that public education is a failure. The forces behind this are neo-conservative think tanks that were largely behind "No Child Left Behind" and its major component, "Reading First." The same kind of campaign has been used in France, Germany, Scotland, England, and other developed countries. Attacking how schools teach literacy is a convenient way to undermine confidence in public education. And that suits business interests who want to minimize tax burdens to educate a population who might vote against their interests. And at the same time, they want to control what literacy is being used for. In developing nations, the World Bank and the International Monetary Fund are putting limits on what can be spent on social programs and education.

Here is the reality: the only illiterates are those who never have access to literacy or those with severe physical or mental disabilities. What we do have are a great many people who, as a result of the way they were taught to read, either:

1.  Learned eventually but never got over considering themselves as inadequate. How many times can you be put in remedial classes where you get more drills on what has never worked for you, before it sinks in there is something wrong with you?
2.  Learned to read well enough to deal with whatever they had to in school, college, and their careers but think of reading as tedious and unpleasant because of a history of uninteresting and unexciting reading instruction.

Adding to this problem of misplaced instruction is the domination of a medical model in programs aimed at remediating the losers. The medical model treats the learner as diseased or defective so the approach is to diagnose some condition which needs to be fixed. Strangely, the fix most always seems to be a large dose of phonics. Partly that's because the assumption is that they failed in the first place because something was missing in them and not because something was wrong with the instructional program. And, of course, this is based on the belief that learning to read is really mastering the skill sequence.

Actually the ability to learn language is so powerful that in most cases it overcomes the effects of misdirected instruction. The common-sense notion that the solution to the problem of kids not learning to read and write is to teach more rigorously and more explicitly a highly sequenced set of skills exacerbates the problem because it is directly opposite to how language is most easily learned. And in the current political atmosphere, some really absurd programs are being imposed on teachers and learners because they promise quick cures. So strong is the notion that reading is the sequence of skills that competent readers—even in secondary schools—are subject to absurd remedial reading programs because they score below the norm on skill tests.

Those who have learned to consider themselves non-readers have the same universal ability as any others to learn and use language but just as schools need to revalue the reading process and how it is best learned, the losers in the skill based programs need to revalue themselves as readers. Many suffer with what I call the next-word-syndrome. They have been taught that good reading is getting the words right. So they come to believe any troublesome words are proof of their inability. They learn to read enough to take care of daily personal responsibilities or job requirements and do not consider what they do read as reading because they never were successful at learning to read in school. I call what is being imposed politically on our schools "The Pedagogy of the Absurd." Scientific knowledge is legally banned and nonsense is framed as Scientific Reading Research.

## Revaluing

For discouraged readers, their teachers and their parents must revalue them as learners and the learners must revalue

 It would be great to see collaboration between educators and Silicon Valley to produce or modify devices that would serve to support the expansion of literacy development in schools. There is considerable potential for adapting current technology for promotion of literacy. For example: a cell phone designed for young hands and minds—not a full function smart phone nor a toy but one that would give very young children access to texting and games involving language and simple problem solving.

More ambitiously: a limited mini-computer or Ipad type of device designed for use in primary classrooms:

- It would have access to an e-library. That would expand the reading/writing they learn in texting and email to enjoyment of story and exposure to affective aspects of literature.
- It would have an app to assist with use for researching and accessing information.
- It would provide apps for aid in translating the language of

themselves as learners. Then the process of reading must be revalued not as the applications of skills to word identification but as a process of meaning making.

Miscue analysis is an easily learned tool for getting both teachers and readers to revalue what happens while reading because it shows the productive strategies even the most troubled readers are using. We have been particularly successful with *retrospective miscue analysis* (Goodman, Martens and Flurkey, 2014). The reader listens to a digital recording of his or her own reading. The teacher selects some miscues or self-corrections that demonstrate the reader's productive use of strategies. Then the reader is asked to recall the thinking that led to the miscue or correction. Sometimes this is done in small groups so all students become knowledgeable about the reading process.

- word problems into operations.
- Apps for different meanings of numbers: in measurement, scaling, counting, sharing, buying, and selling.
- It could provide help in spelling, punctuation, and page formatting.
- It would facilitate email and texting.
- It could provide a child friendly social network (perhaps limited to the classroom).

## Access Is a Key Aspect of All Kinds of Language Development

Perhaps the most important limitation on promoting natural development of literacy is access to the internet and the digital world that exists there. There is no better and cheaper way of promoting early literacy than making access universal. It's a better way because it opens *the literacy club* to all learners which in turn would have even the poorest kids coming to school already literate. The costs of making access universal is offset by what we spend on basal readers and tests.

### Digital Literacy Is Real Reading and Real Writing

There needs to be widespread understanding of the significance of early digital experiences in literacy development of very young children. Those children who have access to written language in its interactive forms—texting, email, participatory games, and apps—are quite likely to be comfortably reading and writing with no instruction.

There is a peer culture that develops at a very early age that strongly influences the actions of young learners. And increasingly this is often supported by the digital culture in the home and the community.

A case in point: our housekeeper was planning a trip to Chihuahua in Mexico, where her family still largely lives. She wanted to surprise her grandfather so she was shocked when her aunt, during a phone call, seemed to know all of her plans. Her pre-teen son and daughter had been texting their cousins in Spanish (though neither had ever had any instruction in texting or in writing Spanish) that they would soon be visiting them.

Parents need to be aware that there is indeed something significant about the early interest in connecting through digital devices. They need to provide access where possible and encourage and keep track of their use without taking control away from the learners. At the same time, they should be selective about apps and package programs that do not directly involve the kids in functional use of written language. And they should have books, magazines, and newspapers available for the children to read so that they can expand on what they are doing digitally. Stories are another way of connecting through sharing the pleasure and learning they provide. Parents can encourage their children to write their own stories, greeting cards, shopping lists, and join in daily family literacy experiences. Sometimes, especially when the young learners show interest, parents will provide information about general conventions of spelling and style.

I have a challenge for those who wish to devote part of the fortunes made in cyberspace to education: put your money where it will work best in providing access to digital literacy to everyone. The air is free so the waves that pass through it should be free as well and access should be universal. We don't need money poured into absurdities such as a knockoff of Dynamic Indicators of Basic Early Literacy Skills (DIBELS) (Good et al., 2001), Early Grade Reading Assessment (EGRA) (Grove and Wetterberg, 2011) which is being imposed on nations in Africa, Asia, and Latin America by the World Bank, United States Agency for international Development (USAID), and the Hewlett Foundation to prove that their kids can't read. Imagine testing kids in Senegal in French nonsense syllables. It's happening! The same African children who learned several languages by the time they were five are failing EGRA in grade three.

## The Future of Literacy

Whether or not we have entirely convinced you about written language and how it works, I hope you will agree that it is neither a mystery nor self-evident and that we have come a long way (here I mean all those who have seriously studied making sense of print) in understanding the reading process.

There is still much to be learned about language and how it is used by our brains in connecting with each other and in utilizing the senses to transact with the world. But I think we are at a point where there is a convergence of theory and understandings in how brain, eye, and language relate. It will be increasingly important to understand these relationships as the ways in which our literacy, individually and socially, becomes more complex on the one hand and more powerful on the other.

We, the three authors of this book, remain optimistic that over time good knowledge drives out bad. We are confident that what we are right about will become accepted and used and what we have not fully understood or misunderstood will be clarified. I am personally proud of the insightful and courageous teachers who are putting knowledge to work on behalf of their students, sometimes under very difficult circumstances. And I weep for the children and teachers who suffer from the excesses of the Pedagogy of the Absurd's current literacy policies. I weep for Detroit where much of my research was done, where my children and I were educated, and where like many cities in the United States, 150 years of educational progress has been negated by foolish and mean-spirited interference by politicians and neo-conservative think tanks.

One hope the authors of this book share is that our readers, armed with a knowledge of how reading works and how well equipped children are for learning to read, will not tolerate the teaching of reading as a sequence of skills and vocabulary drills and will join with professionals in demanding instruction which builds on and promotes language development in the context of its use. Call it whole language or call it informed professional teaching, what is needed are school experiences that are challenging, exciting, and full of new opportunities to expand language while learning.

Literacy itself has a bright future but whether that future will be shared by all or limited to those with access is less certain.

Or, as Langston Hughes (1958) put it, the goal is to "dig and be dug in return."

## References

Berliner, D. C. and Biddle, B. J. (1995). *The manufactured crisis: Myths, fraud, and the attack on America's public schools.* Reading, MA: Addison-Wesley.

Bullock, A. (1975). *The Bullock Report – A language for life: Report of the committee of inquiry.* London: H.M.S.O.

Cole, M., John-Steiner, V. Scribner, S. and Sauberman, E. (Eds). (1978). *Mind in society: The development of higher psychological processes.* Cambridge, MA: Harvard University.

Dewey, J. (1938). *Experience and education.* New York: Macmillan.

Good, R. H., Oregon School Study Council, and Educational Resources Information Center (U.S.). (2001). *Using dynamic indicators of basic early literacy skills (DIBELS) in an outcomes-driven model: Steps to reading outcomes.* Eugene, OR: Oregon School Study Council, School Psychology Program, College of Education, University of Oregon.

Goodman, K. S. (1986). *What's whole in whole language?* Portsmouth, NH: Heinemann.

Goodman, Y. M., Martens, P. and Flurkey, A. (2014). *Retrospective miscue analysis: A window into readers' thinking.* Katonah, NY: Richard C. Owen.

Grove, A. and Wetterberg, A. (Eds.), (2011). *The early grade reading assessment: Applications and interventions to improve basic literacy.* RTI Press Book Series. Research Triangle Park, NC: Research Triangle Institute.

Halliday, M. A. K. (2004). "Three aspects of children's language development: Learning language, learning through language, learning about language." In Webster, J. (Ed.), *The language of early childhood. Volume 4 in the collected works of M.A.K. Halliday* (pp. 308–326). New York: Continuum.

Hughes, L. (1958). *The Langston Hughes reader.* New York: G. Braziller, p. 98.

Smith, F. (1973). "Twelve ways to make learning to read difficult." In Smith, F. (Ed.), *Psycholinguistics and reading* (pp. 183–200). New York: Holt, Rhinehart and Winston.

Smith, F. (1988). *Joining the literacy club: Further essays into education.* Portsmouth, NH: Heinemann.

Spencer, M. M. (1987). *How texts teach what the readers learn.* Victoria, British Colombia: Abel Press.

Thorndike, E. L. (1931). *A teacher's word book of the twenty thousand words found most frequently and widely in general reading for children and young people.* New York: Teachers College Press.

Wilde, S. (Ed.) (1996). *Notes from a kidwatcher: Selected writings of Yetta M. Goodman.* Portsmouth, NH: Heinemann.

# Index